Life And Times Of Bishop William Morgan: The Translator Of The Bible Into The Welsh Language... – Primary Source Edition

William Hughes (Vicar of Llanuwchllyn, Bala.)

LIFE AND TIMES

OF

BISHOP WILLIAM MORGAN.

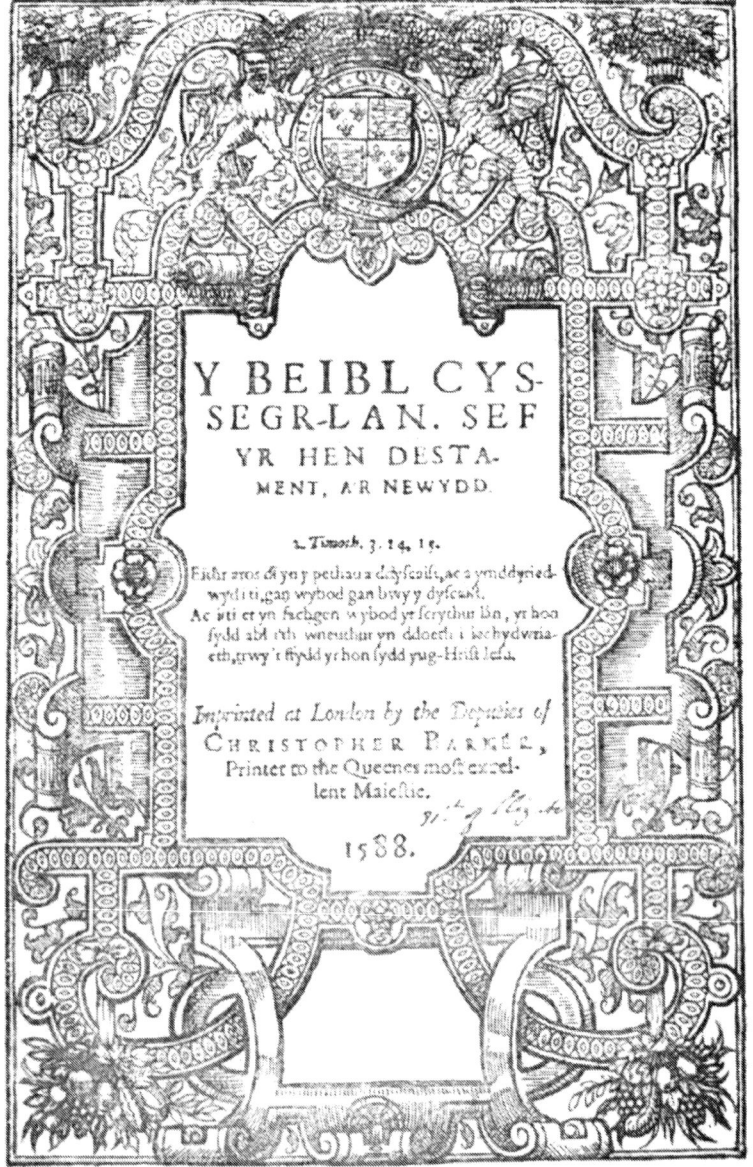

Facsimile of Title-page of Welsh Bible. Engraved, by permission of the Dean of Westminster, from the copy presented by Bishop Morgan himself to the Dean and Chapter of Westminster, and now in the Abbey Library. See p. 121.

.LIFE AND TIMES

OF

BISHOP WILLIAM MORGAN,

THE TRANSLATOR OF THE BIBLE INTO THE WELSH LANGUAGE.

.

BY

THE REV. WILLIAM HUGHES,

VICAR OF LLANUWCHLLYN, BALA ;

JOINT HONORARY SECRETARY OF THE WELSH BIBLE TERCENTENARY COMMEMOR-
ATION FUND ; EDITOR OF "LIFE AND SPEECHES OF DEAN COTTON,"
"LIFE AND LETTERS OF REV. T. CHARLES, BALA," "HANES YR
ESGOB MORGAN," "TYSTIOLAETHAU YMNEILLDUWYR A
THREFNYDDION O BLAID EGLWYS LOEGR," ETC

PUBLISHED UNDER THE DIRECTION OF THE TRACT COMMITTEE.

SOCIETY FOR PROMOTING CHRISTIAN KNOWLEDGE,
LONDON : NORTHUMBERLAND AVENUE, W.C. ;
43. QUEEN VICTORIA STREET, E.C.
BRIGHTON: 135, NORTH STREET.
NEW YORK: E. & J. B. YOUNG & CO.
1891

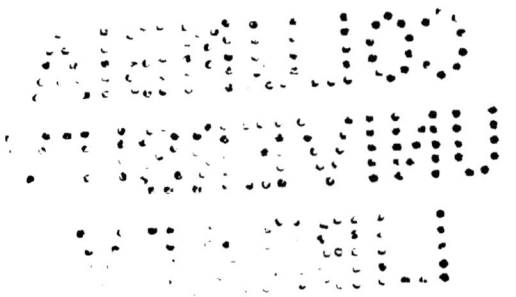

TO

EDWARD WHITE,

LORD ARCHBISHOP OF CANTERBURY,

PRIMATE OF ALL ENGLAND;

A SUCCESSOR TO WHITGIFT, WHOSE LIBERALITY IN A.D. 1588

FIRST GAVE THE BIBLE IN THE VERNACULAR TO THE

CHURCH IN WALES;

AND TO

WILLIAM BASIL, LORD BISHOP OF S. DAVID'S; RICHARD,

LORD BISHOP OF LLANDAFF; ALFRED GEORGE,

LORD BISHOP OF S. ASAPH;

AND DANIEL LEWIS, LORD BISHOP OF BANGOR:

THE LIVING REPRESENTATIVES OF

THE ANCIENT BRITISH CHURCH,

THIS LIFE

OF ONE OF THE GREATEST OF HER LONG SUCCESSION OF

BISHOPS

Is Dedicated,

WITH PROFOUND RESPECT FOR THEIR APOSTOLIC OFFICE

PREFACE.

So little is known of the story of Bishop Morgan's life, that it is impossible, at this distance of time, to draw a full biographical portrait of him. The few documents that exist in the Public Record Office, the British Museum, and Lambeth Palace Library, —copies and photographs of which, by the kind permission of the authorities, I have been able to obtain—form the only exceptions to the almost uniform absence of any discoverable documents bearing on the history of the great Bishop's life.

The Society which has undertaken to publish this work has been the constant friend of Welsh literature, and for the last hundred and seventy-two years has published millions of Welsh Bibles; the Society which supplied the circulating Schools of Griffith Jones, Llanddowror, with Welsh Bibles, in which so many thousands of young and old were taught to read, mark, learn, and inwardly digest God's Holy Word in the vernacular language of Wales.

The writer would fain hope that the publication of this volume may throw some additional light on the life and work of its great subject, and, in a measure, help the reader to realize the moral, religious, and social influences which his labours have reflected on Welsh-speaking people throughout the world.

"A Gair Duw yu uchaf." [1]

Lianuwchllyn,
   May 9, 1891.

---

[1] " And the word of God uppermost."

CONTENTS.

PART I.

INTRODUCTION.

CHAPTER I.

CHAPTER II.

CHAPTER III.

EARLY DAYS.

PART II.

CHAPTER IX.

CHAPTER X.

CHAPTER XI.

CHAPTER XII.

CHAPTER XIII.

LIST OF ILLUSTRATIONS.

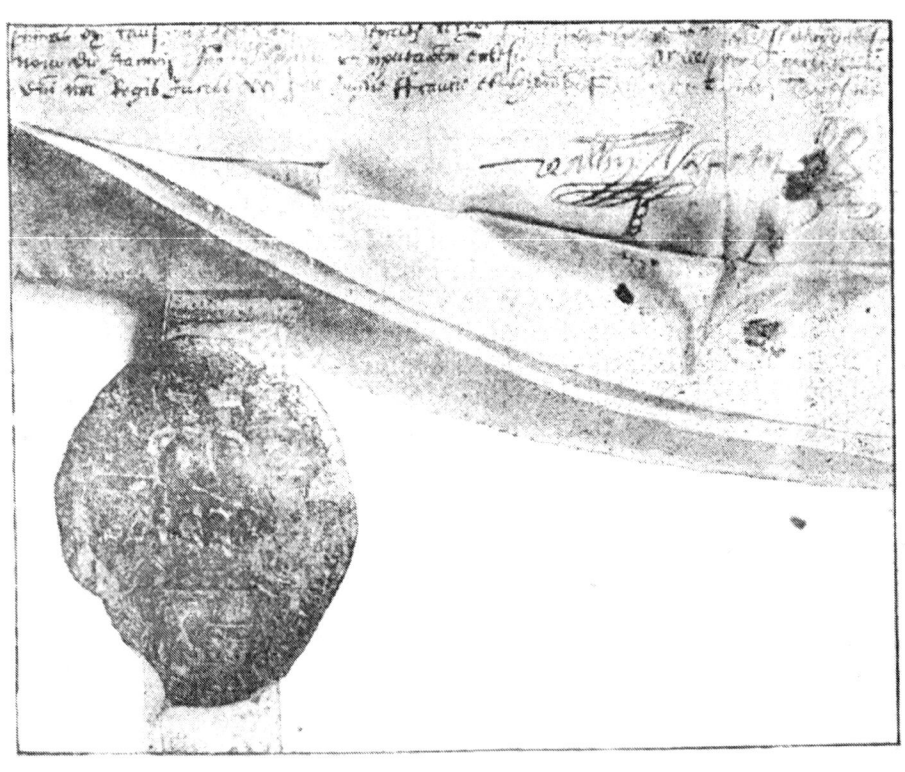

Bishop Morgan's Seal and Autograph.—See p. 186.

LIFE AND TIMES OF BISHOP MORGAN.

PART I.—1547 TO 1567.

INTRODUCTORY CHAPTER.

The Reformation—Papal Supremacy—The Welsh Church and the
Province of Canterbury—Penal Statutes against the Welsh—The
Tudors—"Defender of the Faith"—Revival of the Eisteddfod
—Welsh Legislation—The Use of the Welsh Language in Law
Courts—Used as a Means of furthering the Cause of the Reform-
ation—Lords Marches of Wales—Dissolution of the Monasteries
—Their Moral Condition—State of the Welsh Language at this
Time—Welsh Superstition—Pre-Reformation Translations of the
Bible into Welsh—Dafydd Ddu o Hiraddug—Bishop Goldwell
—William Salesbury.

THE life and times of Bishop Morgan are co-
incident with some of the most memorable events
in the civil and religious history of England and
Wales; and contemporaneous with great epochs
in the history of Christendom. Born about the
close of the reign of Henry VIII., William Morgan witnessed the separation of the Church of
England from the Church of Rome, and lived to
see a strong line of demarcation drawn between the
two Churches in this country. This was the rejection of Papal supremacy; the recovery of the
power of the British Crown over the clergy as

well as over the laity; the introduction of the
English liturgy; the abolition of certain super-
stitious religious practices; the putting forth of the
XXXIX. Articles of Religion; and the unrestricted
use of the Bible.   This is known in history as the
Reformation; the aim of which was, speaking
broadly, to place our religious liberties on a basis
analogous to that on which our civil liberties had
been placed long before.   A supremacy of power
in making and administering Church law was
vested in the Sovereign; but in making Church law
he was to ratify the acts of the Church herself, as
represented in Convocation; and when the highest
civil sanction was necessary, Parliament could be
appealed to.   In administering Church law the
Sovereign was to discharge this function through
the medium of bishops and divines, canons and
civilians, as her own most fully authorized, best
instructed sons.

The Church before the Reformation and the
Church after the Reformation is one; just as a
man who has survived a severe operation—weakened by the shock, it may be—needing time and
care to enable him to recruit his strength—is still
the same man, with the same heart beating, the
same brain working, the same bodily and mental
powers.

In connection with the religious history of
Wales, the study of its archæology is interesting
and instructive.   With all its religious changes the
parochial topography of the country remains much
the same as it was in Morgan's time.   Although a
large number of Welsh parishes bear the name of
the Blessed Virgin—as may be seen in its many

Llanfairs (S. Mary), in consequence of the powerful influence in Wales of the Cistercian Order—it
can be proved that nearly one-half of them had
Welsh saints for their original founders.[1] The
church of Welshpool—the very parish of which
Morgan first became Vicar—is a case in point.
Before, and during his time, this church was known
as S. Mary's, and is still so named; but it was
originally dedicated under the name of S. Cynfelyn
—the founder. The early British Church had her
own saints; her own episcopate; had churches of
her own built after a fashion of her own; and
regarded with great jealousy any ecclesiastical
interference on the part of the Anglo-Saxon
Church. The absorption of Wales in the province
of Canterbury in the twelfth century tended to the
obliteration of the identity of the Welsh Church.
To compensate her, in some degree, for an apparent
surrender, Pope Calixtus dignified David, the
patron saint of Wales, with the title of "Saint,"
A.D. 1115, and he is the only Welsh saint included
in the Western Calendar.

No attempt appears to have been made by the
Archbishop of Canterbury to exercise any jurisdiction in Wales till the year 1188, when Baldwin
made a tour through the Principality, professedly
to preach the Crusades, but really to assert the
archiepiscopal jurisdiction of Canterbury in Wales.
This he did by officiating at the High Altar in the
four Welsh cathedrals. About a century later,
however, there could be no doubt as to that being
one of the objects of Archbishop Peckham, when

[1] *Welsh Saints* (Rees), p. 69.

B

he held an official Visitation of all the Welsh dioceses, A.D. 1284.

The accession of the Welsh House of Tudor to the throne of England, A.D. 1485, in the person of Henry VII. forms a new era in the history of Wales. The harsh enactments of Henry IV., as regards the principality, were not however repealed till the reign of Henry VIII. Next to that of the Reformation, the subject of reform in Wales engaged the king's attention.

True to the instincts of his Welsh character—instincts which have characterized Welshmen from the time of Pelagius to the present day—Henry showed his fondness for theological controversy in his work, *Assertio Septem Sacramentorum adversus Martin Luther.* For this apology Pope Leo X. conferred on the king the title of *Fidei Defensor*—a title which the Pope afterwards regretted he had conferred, and which he endeavoured to withdraw. Parliament, however, ratified it; and all the sovereigns of England have ever since adopted the title, and it is unto this day inscribed on all public documents, and on the coinage of the realm.

The year 1519 marks the revival of Eisteddfodau. This movement gave a decided impetus to Welsh literature. Cambrian bibliography dates from 1546. But there are MSS. anterior to this in the British Museum, the Mostyn, Peniarth, Wynnstay, and other libraries. The greater number have, however, perished. By command of Henry VIII. a royal Eisteddfod was held at Caerwys in 1523.

On a petition of the Welsh people in 1536, a law was passed which in its main provisions enacted: (1) That the principality and country of Wales should be united and incorporated for ever with the Kingdom of England; (2) that all Welsh people should enjoy equal freedom, rights, privileges, and laws with the English subjects of the king without distinction; (3) that lands in Wales should be possessed by the eldest son, according to the English rule of heritage, and not be divided among all the children according to the old Welsh laws; (4) that four Welsh shires should be arranged from the territory which was not so divided before, viz. Radnor, Brecon, Montgomery, and Denbigh; (5) that the lands of the Lords of the Marches be united and joined in part with some English counties, and in part with Welsh counties according to proximity and convenience; (6) that the English language alone be used in all the law courts, and that no one who used the Welsh language should hold any office under the king, under pain of deprivation, until he adopted the use of the English language; (7) that a commission be appointed to divide some counties into hundreds, and enquire into such Welsh laws and customs as it might be profitable to retain; (8) that each one of the twelve shires of Wales have power to return a knight to represent it in the English Parliament, and that every town mentioned in that Act have a similar right to return one burgess to represent it in Parliament; (9) that the knights and burgesses be elected according to the English rule.[1]

The people of Wales were, by this Act of Parliament, put on political equality with the people of

---

[1] 27 Hen. VIII. Act xxvi. *Statutes at Large* (Ed. 1763), vol. ii. pp. 420, 427.

England ; but the use of the English language in the law courts in Wales was compulsory. While the highest offices of the Church in Wales were, at this time, conferred on Welsh-speaking Welshmen, the exclusive use of the Welsh language was a barrier to the most menial office in the civil courts. The use of the Welsh language in the service of religion was, evidently, encouraged solely as a means of helping on the work of the Reformation in Wales.

The government of Wales by the Lords of the Marches was practically abolished by the Act 27 Hen. VIII. c. 24. Henceforth the king took into his own hands the powers invested in that body, and appointed justices of the peace, sheriffs, and other officers.

Though much was gained by the Reformation, it was attended with great and sad excesses. The dissolution of the monasteries soon followed the rejection of the Papal supremacy, whereby considerable numbers of people were turned adrift, homeless, without any employment or relief. The destruction of the monastic system was a powerful factor in the more effectual crushing of the Papal power in England : inasmuch as the abbots and monks were independent of all civil and ecclesiastical authority, and amenable only to the Pope. The king got appropriated to himself by far the greater portion of the monastic revenues, and sold the abbey lands and tithes, at easy prices, to the nobles and gentry, in order to secure their support to the policy of spoliation. The effect of this on society at large was much the same as would be the case now, if the poor laws, infirmaries, asylums, schools, and public libraries were suddenly abolished. The monasteries were homes for the poor and needy, hospitals for the sick and dying—the monks themselves being skilful physicians, as well as the historians of the times. In almost every monastery not only was a record kept of the transactions of the Society, but the political events of the period were regularly noted. All these were swept away by Henry VIII. The movable goods of religious houses were stolen; the libraries left to the ignorant tiller of the soil, who took possession of them for the sake of the parchment they contained; and the magnificent but dismantled buildings abandoned to the pitiless ravages of the elements.

Unsatisfactory as the moral condition of some of the lesser monasteries was said to be, the visitors praised the regularity of the greater ones. To the credit of these institutions be it added, that it was not found necessary to make any legal provision for the poor, till after the dissolution of the monasteries. The first poor law Act dates from the fifth year of Elizabeth, when William Morgan was about sixteen years of age. The new channel, however, into which public benefactions now began to flow, indicated that there was in the public mind a distrust of the monastic system; for whilst no abbey or priory had been founded for upwards of thirty years before the dissolution of the monasteries, the endowment of schools and colleges was becoming more and more frequent.[1]

The correctness of the theory lately advanced,

[1] Knight's *Life of Dean Colet.*

that the Welsh language was on the point of extinction before the dissolution of the monasteries, may be doubted. The disabilities of the Welsh, in this respect, had been practically removed long before, in the reign of Henry VII. Two Royal Eisteddfodau had been held in 1519 and 1523. The Welsh language was not, probably, as purely spoken then as it is now ; but it was the language of the masses, though its literature was more circumscribed, because but few could read then. The writings of Chaucer show the meagreness of the English language also in pre-Reformation times. The number of Welsh books published at the period of the Reformation was so small, and the number of readers so few, that even the Welsh Bible had little influence on the Welsh people and their language, till after the year 1630—the date of the publication of the first octavo Welsh Bible— and which for a long time afterwards could be read by but a few. Its influence was limited, for the most part, to reading and oral teaching in Welsh in churches. The linguistic influence of the monastic system in Wales, as regards the Welsh language, was far less than the influence of English bishops in Wales. Built as the monasteries were in lonely and unfrequented districts, where no external disturbances could distract attention from prayer and meditation, the inmates held little intercourse with the outside world. Moreover, the fraternity included many foreigners, and French and Italian were as frequently spoken within the walls as English or Welsh. The system, in fact, was, at this time, out of touch with the common people.

The Welsh clung tenaciously to the Church of Rome, which is sufficiently attested by the fact that the annals of the Reformation do not furnish us with the name of a single Welsh martyr. Its progress in Wales was not originally of native growth; but the principality was grafted, as it were, into the tree of the English Reformation, retaining, in many respects, its own individuality. Dr. Edward Powell—a distinguished Welshman— fellow of Oriel College, Oxford; rector of Bledon, and prebendary of Salisbury Cathedral,—a man held in the highest esteem in the University of Oxford, wrote against Luther in 1523, and was a stern opponent of the King's supremacy, for the denying of which he was executed at Smithfield, July 30, 1540.[1]

Several of the Welsh bards of the middle ages attacked the errors of the Church of Rome. Dafydd ap-Gwilym (A.D. 1340)—the Welsh Chaucer —wrote against the monks and the priests of his time with much vigour. The Grey Friar he designated "Y dyn Llygliw" (the mouse-coloured man). Dr. Sion Cent, too (A.D. 1417)—a supposed disciple of Lord Cobham—to whom he refers in one of his poems under the old family name of Oldcastle, wrote much in the same strain—

> "Paid aro, ond cof y cwymp
> Olkaist, ti ai yn eilcwymp."

According to the Welsh Triads, the preaching of the Grey Friar was not popular in Wales:
"Tri pheth ni waeth pa leiaf y clywir o honynt;

[1] Williams' *Eminent Welshmen.*

can hwch ar wynt, cnec hen wrach, a phregeth Brawd Llwyd."

Nor are the Triads less emphatic in their protest against the wafer bread of the Mass, and the veneration of relics—

"Tri pheth ni waeth i ddyn ychydig na llawer o honynt; bara offeren, nawdd y creiriau, a rhoddion mab y crin-was." (Cybydd.)

Gruffydd ap Ieuan ap Llewelyn Fychan, a celebrated Welsh poet, and one of the chief promoters of the Caerwys Royal Eisteddfod in 1523, thus spoke of (1) Angel worship and (2) Image worship—

> (1) " Ni all angel penfelyn
>   Na llu mawr o saint, dim lle in'.
>   Na dim byw wedi eni
>   I'r nef a'n swccria ni,
>   Na neb ond Un a'i Aberth
>   A roes i ni ras a nerth."
>
> (2) " Dyma'r dallder arferwyd,
>   Delwau oedd well na Duw lwydd,
>   Esg'luso Duw byw o'n bodd
>   Mawrhau diawl mawr hudolodd
>   A rhoi addoliant ar ddeulin
>   A ddylai i Grist, i ddelwgrin ;
>   Ffynio Gwenffrewi ffynon
>   Ffiaidd a hyll yw'r ffydd hon."

The literature of Wales suffered much by the destruction of Bangor-is-y-coed monastery, A.D. 613. So important a Christian centre would, doubtless, contain a Welsh translation of some portion of Holy Writ. S. Jerome (A.D. 390) speaks of Britain as "worshipping the same Christ, and observing the same rule of faith as other nations." It is doubtful whether the Latin Vulgate was at any time in use among British Christians.　Haddan and Stubbs[1] quote extracts of Scripture collected from British and Scottish writers, which " agree neither with any other of the ante-Hieronymian versions (unless with those found in British or Irish MSS.) nor with the Vulgate, and which therefore go to establish a presumption that a special variety of the former existed peculiar to the British Isles."　We have it on ·the same authority,[2] " that there is no trace whatever anywhere of any Celtic version of the Bible or any part of it."

The Latin letter of Peckham, Archbishop of Canterbury, A.D. 1282, addressed to the Canons of S. Asaph, authorizing them to use the MS. translation of the Four Gospels then in the Cathedral, is evidence of the existence of a translation, which was considered old even at that time.　But it is impossible to say whether it was a Latin, English, or Welsh version of the Gospels.　The designation " Evengeiython," quoted by Peckham, and probably a corruption of the Welsh " Efengylyddion," or Gospels, does not necessarily prove that it was Welsh.　The Welsh people would call it " Efengyl " (Gospel) in whatever language it was written.　The probabilities are that it was a Latin manuscript, carried about as a relic, but not read to and by the people themselves ; it is supposed to have remained at S. Asaph Cathedral till the time of Bishop Goldwell, deprived at the accession of Elizabeth, for his opposition to the Reformation, who fled to Rome, taking this MS. and other diocesan papers with him.　Browne Willis[3] discredits

---

[1] *Councils*, vol. i. p. 170.　　[2] *Ibid.* vol. i. p. 193.
[3] *Survey*, vol. i. p. 102.

this story, on the authority of a gentleman who told him that he had made a careful search at the Vatican ; that there were no papers of any kind there pertaining to the diocese of S. Asaph. Bishop Richard Davies, Goldwell's successor, makes no reference to the manuscript in his letter prefixed to Salesbury's N. T., which goes far to prove that it was not a Welsh translation, and that it had disappeared long before Goldwell's time ; otherwise Davies could hardly have omitted to make mention of it, especially as he speaks of a Welsh manuscript of the Pentateuch which he saw, when a boy, in the house of his uncle.

Gwallter Mechain[1] speaks of a Welsh MS. translation of the Gospel according to S. John, written on parchment in a fair hand of the style of the twelfth or thirteenth century, which was sold in his time with the library of Mr. J. Lloyd, Hafodunos, and was entitled *Gwaith Ioan Efangylystor*—"The work of John the Evangelist." Dafydd Ddu o Hiraddug, or Dafydd ap Hovel ap Madoc, is said to have translated portions of the Book of Psalms into Welsh about 1349 ; also part of the first chapter of the Gospel according to S. Luke, including the Song of Zacharias and the Salutation of the Angel Gabriel to Mary. He also translated from the Latin into Welsh the *Officium B. Mariæ*, which contains some portions of the Psalms, and is interesting as containing probably the earliest known Welsh translations from the Book of Psalms.[2]

[1] *Gweithiau*, vol. ii. p. 190.
[2] Dafydd Ddu was Vicar of Tremeirchion, and Canon of S. Asaph, about the middle of the fourteenth century. The recumbent effigy of a priest in sacerdotal robes, in the north

Bishop Richard Davies in his letter prefixed to Salesbury's N. T. says—

"I never saw a Welsh Bible; but when I was a boy, I remember seeing the five books of Moses in Welsh in my uncle's house, who was a learned man, but no one paid any attention to the book, nor put any value upon it.[1] I am doubtful if it be possible to see any old Welsh Bible in the whole of Wales. But I have no doubt that the Welsh Bible was at one time common enough. The perfection of the faith of the martyrs, clerical and lay, is a strong proof that they had the Holy Scriptures in their own language. . . . We have also in the Welsh language several expressions and proverbs that continue still in use, and are taken from Holy Scriptures, and from the Gospel of Christ. These are sufficient proofs that the Holy Scriptures were in every one's head, when they were begun, and when they were brought into general use. Such proverbs as "Duw a digon, heb Dduw heb ddim" (with God enough, without God without anything); "Mor wired ar Efengyl" (as true as the Gospel), and such other like proverbs. There are also many names formerly in use among the Welsh that afford an additional proof of this: such as Abraham, Bishop of S. David's; Adda

---

wall of the chancel of Tremeirchion Church, and bearing the inscription *Hic Jacet David ap Roderic ap Madog*, is said to be the grave of Dafydd Ddu (Pennant's *Tours*, vol. ii. p. 22). The translations above referred to have been reprinted in the *Myvyrian Archæology*, pp. 367—377.

[1] Dr. Llewelyn, in his *History of the Translation of the Welsh Bible*, p. 3, suggests that Tyndale may have been the translator. But this is mere conjecture.

Fras, one of the bards; Aaron, Bishop of S. Asaph; Daniel, the first Bishop of Bangor; Samuel Beulan, a learned clergyman; Samson, the twenty-sixth and the last Bishop of S. David's, and such-like names that occur in the old pedigrees. These show that the Scriptures were well known among our ancestors."[1]

Foremost in the history of Welsh Reformation literature, stands the name of William Salesbury.

The date and place of his birth are not known to a certainty. In his *Battery of the Pope's Botte-reulx*, published in 1550, he speaks of himself as a "yonge man." Plas-isaf, Llanrwst, is commonly accepted as the place of his birth. A note, how-ever, in Salesbury's own handwriting on a manu-script on Botany in the possession of Ioan Pedr,[2] upsets this theory. It is to this effect, " Llansannan sef y plwyf y ganed fi" (Llansannan, the parish wherein I was born). Cae du, Llansannan, is the rightful claimant, apparently, to the honour of being Salesbury's birthplace. Gwallter Mechain traces Salesbury's genealogy to a Norman source; while another deduces him from Ednyfed Fychan, Chancellor of Llewelyn the Great; and, according

---

[1] A Welsh version of the Bible was preserved in MS. at *Celyd Ifan*, near Bridgend in Glamorgan : it appears to have been executed from the Latin Vulgate by an ancestor of the family residing in that place, about the year 1470. A con-siderable portion of the MS. was still extant a few years ago (1851), and in all probability it is still preserved. It may have been a MS. of the Pentateuch of this Version to which Dr. R. Davies referred. We may, however, also mention that it has been stated that the translation of the Pentateuch into English by William Tyndale, was the basis of a Welsh translation" (*The Bible of Every Land*, p. 131).

[2] *Arch. Cambr.*, vol. iii. (Fourth Series) p. 360.

to Sir John Wyn,[1] the family settled at Lleweni, Denbighshire. His grandfather, Robert Salesbury Hên, of Lleweni, the head of the family, obtained the Plas-isaf estate by marriage with Gwenhwyvar, daughter of Rhys ab Einion Vychan. Salesbury was educated in his native county of Denbigh. He was at Oxford "either in S. Alban's or Broadgate Hall, or both," says Wood (*Athen. Oxon.*). Two Welshmen, John Williams and John Ap Harry, were principals of Broadgate Hall between 1540 and 1550. This is probably the period in which Salesbury was at Oxford. The principles of the Reformation had taken root at the University before Salesbury's time, and he was at Oxford between 1540 and 1547, when Peter Martyr and Jewel were the leaders of thought there. In his *Battery*, Salesbury thus speaks of himself when a Roman Catholic.[2] "As I was thus tangled and abominablye deceyved, and trayned, and brought up in tender age in the Pope's holilyke Religion before Christes second byrthe here in England."

A translation into Welsh, by Sir John Price, of the *Institutions of the Christian Man*, or the *Bishop's Book*, appeared in 1546. This was the first book ever printed in the Welsh language, and had the following title: "Bibl : yn y Llyvyr hwn y traethyr Gwyddor Cymraeg. Kalendyr. Y Gredo, neu bynkeu y ffydd Gatholig. Y Pader, neu Weddi

[1] *Memoirs*, p. 39.
[2] Salesbury's great-uncle, Ffoulk Salesbury, was Dean of S. Asaph's from 1511 to 1543. He was also rector of Llanrhaiadr and Llandyrnog, and prebendary of Llanfair in the Cathedral of Bangor, and was the first Dean of S. Asaph to renounce the Papal supremacy.

yr Arglwydd. Y Deng Air Deddyf. Y Kampay
arferadwy a'r Gweddiau gocheladwy ac Keingeu."

The lack of a Welsh dictionary added to the
difficulty, at this time, of translating into the Welsh
language. To supply this defect Salesbury published in 1547 "A Dictionary in Englyshe and
Welshe, moche necessary to all such Welshemen as
will spedly learne the Englyshe tongue, thought
unto the Kynges majestie very mete to be sette
forth to the use of his grace's subjects ; whereunto
is prefixed a little treatyse of the Englyshe pro-
nunciacion of the letters." There was at this time
no Welsh literature worthy of the name, and the
materials for a vocabulary were scanty indeed. The
rebellion of Owain Glyndwr ; the Wars of the
Roses, and the destruction of the monasteries
involved the ruin of almost all collections of Welsh
MSS. whether in the possession of ecclesiastical
bodies, or of private individuals. Salesbury does
not appear to have obtained possession of any
monastic MSS., and was obliged to trust largely
to his own memory, as well as that of others for
his collection of Welsh words. The Dictionary
contains 5500 words, out of which number 1200
bear the marks of the influence of the English
language. In his Dedication of the work to Henry
VIII. Salesbury says : "Wherefore, seeing there is
many of your grace's subjects in Wales that readeth
perfectly the Welsh tongue, which, if they had
English expounded in the Welsh speech, might be
both their own schoolmasters and other men's also,
and thereby most speedily obtain the knowledge of
the English tongue throughout all the country. I
have writ a little English Dictionary with the

Welsh interpretation, whereunto I have prefixed a treatise of the English pronunciation of the letters."

This extract is a clear testimony to the fact that there was, at the time, a sufficient number of people able to read Welsh as to justify the publication of a Welsh dictionary; which was, however, compiled, as Salesbury says, with the idea of extending thereby a knowledge of English, through the medium of the Welsh, without any intention of prolonging the existence of the latter. Salesbury himself was a man of gentle birth, and English was then, as now, the language of the upper classes in Wales, and his knowledge of Welsh was acquired comparatively late in life. His sympathies would be largely with the English, as the language of his home, and the one he spoke and understood best.

The history of the birth, home, and early associations of William Morgan, differs widely from that of Salesbury, as we shall see in the next chapter.

CHAPTER I.

BIRTH AND EARLY YEARS.

A.D. 1547—1558.

EDWARD VI. AND MARY, 1547—1558.

ARCHBISHOPS OF CANTERBURY.

THOMAS CRANMER,   1533—1555
REGINALD POLE,   1555—1558

BISHOPS OF S. ASAPH.	*BISHOPS OF BANGOR.*
ROBERT WARTON, 1536—1556	ARTHUR BULKELEY, 1542—1555
THOMAS GOLDWELL, 1556—1560	WILLIAM GLYNN, 1555—1559

BISHOPS OF S. DAVID'S.	*BISHOP OF LLANDAFF.*
WILLIAM BARLOW, 1536—1548	ANTHONY KITCHIN, 1545—1566
ROBERT FERRAR, 1548—1554	
HENRY MORGAN, 1554—1560	

Birth of William Morgan—His Coat-of-Arms—Morgan's Ancestors and Descendants—Parish of Penmachno—Local Traditions— Ty Mawr—Gwibernant—The Parish Church of Penmachno —Morgan's Early Education — A Local Tradition — Gwydir Chaplain.

WILLIAM MORGAN was born at Ty Mawr, a farm-house in the parish of Penmachno, Carnarvon-shire, situate at the top of the dingle through which the brook Gwibernant runs.

The exact date of his birth is not known. The years 1541, 1543, and 1547 are commonly given. The year 1547 being, probably, the correct one.

The "Catalogus Episcoporum Qui e Collegio Divi Joannis Evangelistæ prodierunt" in the *History of St. John's College, Cambridge,*[1] vol. i. p. 253, has the following entry—

"Gulielmus Morgan, vel Morgayne Wallus, natus apud Gwibernant in parochia de Penmachno diocesis Bangor. et com. Carnarvon, filius Joannis Morgan ex antiqua familia ibidem, notus in patrium animo paterno."

Bishop Humphreys, of Bangor, sent the following account of Morgan, in a letter to Ant. A. Wood, May, 1692.

"William Morgan, that incomparable man for piety and industry, zeal for religion and his country, and a conscientious care of his Church and succession, was born at a place called Gwibernant in the parish of Penmachno. Diocesse of Bangor and Com. Carnarvon, and was the son of John Morgan of that place (paternally descended from Hedd Moelwynog, one of the fifteen tribes of North Wales)[2] and of his wife Lowry, daughter of William ap John ap Madoc ap Evan Jeyin of

---

[1] 1869. Edited by Prof. Mayor. (Cambridge University Press.)

[2] The five Regal tribes which were of North and South Wales, and the respective representative of each, were considered as of royal blood. The fifteen Common tribes, all of North Wales, and the respective representative of each, formed the nobility, were lords of distinct districts, and held some hereditary office in the palace. By the laws of Hywel Dda there were twenty-four great officers of the Welsh Court. (YORKE's *Royal Tribes of Wales,* p. 1.)

C

Bettws; paternally from Marchiedd, another of the fifteen tribes."[1]

Pennant[2] deduces the Morgans of Gwibernant, and consequently William Morgan, from Nevydd Hardd,[3] the sixth tribe of North Wales. The coat of Nevydd Hardd was "Argent, three spears heads *sable* pointed upwards, *imbrued gules*."

Randle Holmes, the compiler of Harl. 1974, Deputy-Herald under the Heralds' College for North Wales and Cheshire, who lived nearly contemporary with Morgan, must be the most trustworthy authority on this point. He gives, "Sable, a hart passant argent attired and hoofed or." This is probably the correct coat of the family; and is in the Hedd Moelwynog line.

Morgan's own coat, as appears from his official seal in the Record Office, was blazoned per-fess— and Or; in chief an open book, in base an imperial eagle (or, an eagle bilapitate displayed, sable). He, probably, adopted the coat of his eminent ancestor, Meyrick Llwyd, from Hedd Moelwynog, which was an eagle displayed, with two heads, sable; the book probably representing an open Welsh Bible, which Morgan adopted on his elevation to the Episcopate. His pedigree is given on folio 132 of the second division of the MS. transcript volume of Pedigrees (*Harleian Miscellany*, 1794) in the British Museum, and which shows William to be the youngest of five children, viz. Morris, Elizabeth, Morgan ap John, and Jaune— two brothers and two sisters.

[1] Lansdowne MS. in British Museum 983, f. 40.
[2] *Tours in Wales* (Rhys Edition), vol. iii. Appendix, p. 436.
[3] So also Yorke in his *Royal Tribes*, p. 101.

As Bishop Morgan left no issue of his marriage, there were no direct descendants, though some have claimed relationship in a direct line from him. A brother lived at Penmachno, after the Bishop's death, who had sons and daughters. There were no doubt three descendants in a lateral line living at Penmachno, in the latter part of the last century: (1) Ellen Ellis Morgan, who married Arthur Jones of the Lower Mill, Llanrwst, and by whom she had, among other children, Arthur Jones of Bangor; (2) William Ellis Morgan, a brother; and (3) John Ellis Morgan, another brother, whose daughter Elizabeth Ellis Morgan, by Catharine his wife, was baptized at Penmachno parish church on the 23rd of April, 1786.[1]

Morgan was the first of the family to drop the ap in his name, and to adopt the surname Morgan.

[1] "Bye-Gones," in Oswestry *Advertizer*, April 6, 1887. The following note also appears under the same heading, in the issue of the same paper for August 3, 1887 : " I have had put into my hand to-day a document relating to Bishop Wm. Morgan's family. It says, ' Ellis Morgan was fourth in descent from Evan Morgan (Wm. Morgan's nephew), and had by his wife Ellen, (1) John; (2) William; (3) Griffith; (4) Robert. The last named married Gaenor Isaac, and had two sons, to be mentioned: *William*, who, by his wife Gwen, had three children, Rhys, Catherine, Ellis; *Robert*, by his wife, Mary Lloyd, had: Ellen, John, Elizabeth, Robert, and their baptisms can be verified. Ellis Morgan, who heads the list, resided at Doly-ddelan, and was a sort of general dealer there. His son John dwelt at Penmachno, and companionated much with the clergy of his day, and acted the part of a lay attorney in settling disputes between neighbours. The second son William was an old man when his father died, and he was a zealous churchman, just at the time when Methodism began to spread in the neighbourhood of Bettws-y-coed, Penmachno and Doly-ddelan.' "

It had now become the fashion in Wales, as in England, to adopt surnames.

Sir John Wyn says that Morgan was born "at Dolwyddelen, in the Comot of Nant Conway, and County of Carnarvon; descended from the race of the bondmen of that town, servants (both he and his ancestors) to the house of Gwydyr, where he was brought up in learning."[1]

Penmachno is situate in the hundred of Nant Conway, and derives its name from its situation at the source of the river Machno—*i.e.* Pen, or top, of the Machno—which rises in the south-west of the parish, flows through it in a north-easterly direction, and falls into the Conway; which also has its source in a lake of the same name in this parish. The river Conway, where it divides the counties of Carnarvon and Denbigh, fringes the border of Penmachno parish for about three miles. The surface of the parish is mountainous; the soil in the valleys fertile, and the lands, which are watered by the Machno and other streams that descend from the hills, are productive, and in a good state of cultivation.

The view from the higher ground of Bwlch-y-groes, which stands a little distance behind Ty Mawr, extends over a wide tract of country, abounding in picturesque beauty, embracing the Carnarvonshire, Denbighshire, and Merionethshire mountains. To the north-west, just over the shoulder of Bwlch-y-groes, stand Moel Siabod and the Glyders, and, in a more northerly direction, Carnedd Llewelyn and Carnedd Ddafydd. Almost due west, on the far horizon, Snowdon, like a

[1] *Memoirs*, p. 95.

crowned monarch, towers above them all. Looking north-east from the doorway of Ty Mawr, the Hiraethog mountains, with their lights and shades of green, brown heath and shaggy wood, also present a fine landscape—a scenery which Morgan must have frequently enjoyed from the doorway of his humble home, and as he ascended the slopes of the Ty Mawr sheepwalk on Bwlch-y-groes. There are some local traditions at Penmachno connected with this mountain, which are interesting; but possibly not trustworthy.

In Morgan's time Bwlch-y-groes was much frequented, but now the green grass grows thickly over the once well-trodden path. Upon one spot of the Bwlch, about two miles above Ty Mawr, were to be seen, at one time, the *meini cred,* or Creed-stones, into which was incised, it is said, the sign of the cross. It was customary among Welsh people then to cross themselves when going on a journey. "Ymgroesa, Ymgroesa"[1] (cross thyself, cross thyself), was the admonition not only to every one entering on a journey, but on all important occasions, and implied a sense of temptation or danger, "be on your guard, remind yourself of the holy sign," *i.e.* do not do it. It was also a custom to mark sheep with the sign of the cross, and the top of doorways, as also the steeples of churches, so as to be conspicuous to the

---

[1] A custom still prevails, and is a very common one among the Welsh peasantry, of making the sign of the cross on the flour after the barm has been put in it for kneading—called in Welsh "heplas"—a term said to be derived from the words which the women used to say, when making the sign of the cross, "Heb ras, *heb-les*" (without grace, without good); hence the term "heplas."

view of wayfarers. The provision on Bwlch-y-groes
was two Creedstones, placed on either side of the
narrow path, so that the traveller, kneeling between
them, could place his hands on the stones, and his
fingers in the sign of the cross. The arms of the
crosses were said to be about four or five inches in
length, and half an inch wide; so that the wayfarer
could feel them at night, in his perilous journey.
Tradition has it that Morgan's mother used to say:
"I expect great things from my son William: there
never was any one more careful than he to say his
paternosters (paderau) by the Creedstones."[1]   The
stones, which were much disfigured with letters cut
into them by pilgrims, cannot now be found, and
exist only in the local traditions of Penmachno.
They were, probably, put up originally by the
Knights of S. John of Jerusalem, who had a hospital in the neighbouring parish of Yspytty, and
had made its precincts a sanctuary.[2]

Ty Mawr stands on the Penmachno side of the
Gwibernant, the stream which divides that parish
from Dolwyddelen. Very little, if any, remains of
the original building, though its general features
are, probably, the same as they were when Morgan
first breathed under its roof.[3]   Time has effected

[1] *Gweithiau Gethin*, p. 391. (Llanrwst, 1884.)
[2] Pennant's *Tours*, vol. ii. p. 131.
[3] The present house is a modern building, but there are
traces in its walls of two former buildings of different periods.
Up to the year 1806 the house bore the inscriptions over the
doorway, "Heb Dduw, heb dim"; "Duw a digon";—
"Without God, without anything"; "God and enough." The
house now belongs to Lord Penrhyn, who repaired it in 1884,
after it had remained in ruins for a long time, and is now
occupied.   A slab, with marble border, was then put over the

considerable changes on the handiwork of man in Ty Mawr, but the surrounding scenery remains unchanged, connecting the past with the present, and taking us back to the time of Morgan's boyhood, when he used to play on the slopes of the hilly ground above Ty Mawr.

The associations are all of the humblest character ; and the very scene of his birthplace seemed connected with memories of poverty and toil.

The name " Gwibernant " is variously spelt and derived. " Wibernant," " Ewybyrnant," " Gwibernant." Morgan spelt it " Wybernant," and he would be the best authority on the subject. Sometimes the word is spelt " Wy-y-fer-nant," *i. e.* Afon-y-nant fer, or the river of the short dingle. Gwy is the same as river, and nant is the word used in Carnarvonshire for a dingle, or a pass between two mountains, *e. g.* Nant-Ffrancon. But in Merionethshire, nant is the name generally given for a brook. This seems a natural derivation : the " nant," or the dingle, and the " gwy," or the river, both being short as compared to the other dingles in the neighbourhood, and the rivers that flow into the Conway. Nant-y-dwfr peraidd is another derivation, *i. e.* the dingle of the sweet water, from the supposed special sweetness of the water of this particular brook. Another traditional derivation is " Gwibernant," or the dingle of the serpent; from the tradition that there was here at one time a winged

---

doorway outside, bearing the following inscription : " In this house was born William Morgan, D.D., Bishop of St. Asaph. He first translated the entire Bible into Welsh. Born 1541. Died Sepr. 10th, 1604."

serpent, sometimes crawling, sometimes flying on
the top of the trees, seizing its prey below. Dafydd
Goch Gethin [1] of Fedw Deg, a brave soldier, and a
native of this place, returning from abroad, undertook to destroy the monster. Proceeding as far as
Rhyd-gynen, below Pont-y-pandy, on the brink of
a precipice over a deep pool of water, on the
Machno, he watched his victim. The opportunity
came. Gethin pierced the serpent through with his
bow and arrow; the monster fell into the pool and
perished. Rhydygwenwyn—the Ford-of-the-poison
—the exact spot where this is said to have happened,
is supposed to derive its name from the poison
which oozed out of the carcase. Such is the story
of the serpent.

The present church of Penmachno, built in 1861,
situate about two miles from Ty Mawr, stands
within the same enclosure, but not on the same
spot as the old church which had stood for nearly
700 years before, in which Morgan and his parents
used to worship. Two incised stones of great
antiquity, which formed part of the walls of the old
church, at which Morgan must have often looked,

[1] Dafydd Goch of Penmachno was the son of Dafydd, Lord
of Denbigh, the brother of our last Prince Llewelyn. Prince
David, who resided at Denbigh, was seized near the place by
his own countrymen, and carried laden with irons to Edward
I., then at Rhuddlan ; thence he was taken before the parliament sitting at Shrewsbury. Here Dafydd (the father of our
hero of the serpent) was tried and condemned, and was the
first who suffered the death of a traitor in the form of the
sentence now in use. His head was cut off and, with the
head of his brother Prince Llewelyn, was placed on the highest
pinnacle of the Tower of London. Edward put a wreath of
willow on their heads, because the Welsh people used to love
to crown their princes with willow.

are now at the west end of the present church and in a good state of preservation. The inscriptions are—

℞

(1)
        CARAVSIVS
        HIC IACIT
        IN HOC CON
        CERTES LA
        PIDUM.

(Caravsius lies buried in this heap of stones, *i. e.* Carnedd.) The inscription on the second stone is—

(2)
        CANTIORI HIC IACIT
        VENEDOTI SCIVE FUIT
        CONSOBRINO
        MA . FILI
        T MAGISTRAT,

which indicates that the person buried here was a Venedotian (Gwynedd) citizen. It is said that the word "magistrate" has never been found on any other stones, and this must carry them back to a very early period. The present building has no special interest in connection with the history of Morgan, beyond that a three-light coloured east window was erected in it to his memory in 1863, by public subscription, which reached £120. The sun now shines through the letters of his name, near, if not on the actual spot, wherein William was made a member of Christ, a child of God, and an inheritor of the Kingdom of Heaven. The figures and inscriptions are—

THE ASCENSION.

S. PETER.	S. JOHN THE BAPTIST.	S. PAUL.
He saith unto him again the second time, Simon, son of Jonas, lovest thou me? He saith unto him, Yea, Lord, thou knowest that I love thee. He saith unto him, Feed my sheep. St. John xxi. 16.	For this is he that was spoken of by the Prophet Esias, saying, The voice of one crying in the wilderness. Prepare ye the way of the Lord, make his paths straight. St. Matt. iii. 3.	But God forbid that I should glory, save in the Cross of our Lord Jesus Christ, by whom the world is crucified unto me, and I unto the world. Gal. vi. 14.

"IN MEMORY OF WILLIAM MORGAN, D.D., BISHOP OF ST. ASAPH. BORN IN THIS PARISH. DIED SEPR. 10, 1604."

The Baptismal Registers of Penmachno parish do not go beyond the year 1786. The register in which we may reasonably suppose Morgan's baptism to have been duly entered, suffered the same fate, probably, as most registers in the time of the Commonwealth.

The Liturgy in use at Penmachno church in Morgan's early days was, no doubt, the "Use of Bangor," which was generally adopted in North Wales, as the "Use of Hereford" in South Wales. Shut in from the outer world by its natural environs, we may suppose that the spiritual ministrations in the parish church were not of the highest order at that time. The wave of the Reformation had then scarcely penetrated into the innermost recesses of Wales. The *Book of Homilies* was published in the same year as Morgan was born, as a help to such clergy as were unable to preach, or abstained from doing so, lest they should commit themselves on a point of doctrine. Many, for the latter reason, adopted the custom of writing their sermons. In England, the greater part of the beneficed clergy were mechanics, or "mass-priests" in disguise; many churches were closed, and there was hardly any preaching, in such churches as were open, within a circuit of twenty miles. This was the state of things in England when Morgan was born. Matters were worse in Wales. There were no "helps" to preaching in the Welsh language, for no translation of the *Book of Homilies* appeared till the year 1606. The average acreage of a Welsh parish is more than double that of an English parish. The area of the diocese of S. David's is 2,360,000 acres, which far exceeds that of any other diocese in England or Wales. Add to this the great difficulties of inland communication, especially in mountainous districts like Penmachno. The highways, ill-constructed and indifferently kept, and the only means of transit, were almost impassable during bad weather, and could only be traversed by the pack-horse, or "ceffyl-pwn."

Tradition has it at Penmachno that, when Morgan was about five years old, a monk, said to be related to the family, found a home at Ty Mawr, where he lived in hiding, employing his time in teaching the future Welsh bishop. The fame of the lad's scholastic attainments reached the ears of "Sir" John Wyn of Gwydir, who was in happy ignorance of the source of his training. This was not, it is added, accidental, for "Sir" John was an avowed enemy of the monks.[1] If there is any truth underlying this tradition, it is certainly inaccurate in its details. The person who lived at Gwydir during Morgan's childhood was Maurice Wyn, the father of John Wyn. The son inherited the estate at the death of his father in 1580, and

[1] *Gweithiau Gethin*, p. 388.

was created a baronet in 1611. If there was a monk at all in Ty Mawr, he was actually teaching Morgan when Sir John Wyn was born. The tradition has very little, if any, foundation in fact. The testimony of the latter on the question of Morgan's education is conclusive, for he tells us clearly that he "was brought up in learning at Gwydir."[1] There was scarcely any provision for higher education in Wales at this time, with the exception of the Collegiate School at Brecon, founded by Henry VIII., Bangor Free Grammar School, founded in 1557 by Dr. Geoffrey Glynn, and Shrewsbury School, founded by Edward VI. Morgan could not have profited by these institutions. Other Welsh grammar schools were founded subsequently to the period of his school-days. Carmarthen in 1576 by Elizabeth, on the petition of Bishop Richard Davies and others; Ruthin in 1595 by Dean Goodman; Beaumaris in 1603 by David Hughes; and Hawarden in 1609 by George Ledsham.

The famous letter—half insolent, half pious—addressed by Mr. John Wyn to his chaplain, throws some light on the question of Morgan's early education, and is for that reason inserted here. It is also interesting as affording an insight into the relationship between a chaplain and his master in those days.

"First you shall have the chamber[2] I showed you in

[1] *Memoirs*, p. 95.
[2] "This chamber, and a gloomy one it is, still stands at the entrance to Gwydir, from the Bettws-y-coed road. The gateway (which has the arms and initials of Sir John over it) is perhaps the oldest portion of the place remaining."
Gwydir Memorials, xi.

my gate private to yourself, with lock and key and all necessaries. In the morning I expect you shall rise and say prayers in my hall to my household below, before they go to work, and when they come in at nyght; that you call before you all the workmen, specially to give and take account of them of their belief, and of what Sir Meredith[1] taught them. I beg you to continue for the most part in the lower house;[2] you are to have onlye what is done there that you may inform me of any disorder there. There is a baylyf of husbandry, and a porter, who will be commanded by you. The morninge after you be up, and have said prayers, as afore, I wo^d you to bestow in study, or any commendable exercise of your body. Before dinner you are to com up and attend grace, or prayers, if there be any publicke; and to set up, if there be not greater strangers, above the chyldren—who you are to teach in your chamber. When the table, from half downwards, is taken up, then are you to rise, and to walk in the alleys near at hand, until grace time; and to come in then for that purpose. After dinner, if I be busy, you may go to bowles, shuffel bord, or any other honest decent recreation, until I go abroad. If you see me voyd of business, and go to ride abroad, you shall command a geldinge to be made ready by the grooms of the stable, and to go with me. If I go to bowles, or shuffel bord, I shall lyke of your company, if

---

[1] This was probably a neighbouring clergyman. "Sir" was a title formerly bestowed on the clergy, the beneficed clergy at least, as now upon knights, *e. g.* "Sir Hugh Evans," the Welsh parson in the *Merry Wives of Windsor.* The rector of Llanrwst about this time was George Lloyd, B.D., who in 1599 became Bishop of the Isle of Man, from whence he was translated to Chester in 1604. His father was Meredith Lloyd, of Carnarvonshire (Browne Willis, *Hist. Dio. St. Asaph*, vol. i. p. 345). Sir John probably mistook the father's name for that of the son.
[2] Lower Gwydir.

the place be not made up with strangers.   I would have
you go every Sunday in the year to some church here-
abouts, to preache, giving warnynge to the parish to
bring the youths at after noon to the church to be cate-
kysed ; in which poynt is my greatest care that you
be paynfull and diligent.   Avoyd the ale-house, to sytt
and keepe drunkards company ther, being the greatest
discredit your function can have."

Morgan was not, of course, among those children
whom the Gwydir chaplain was commanded to
"teach in his own chamber."   But it is almost
certain that he was one of a former generation of
pupils, in the time of John Wyn's father.   This
seems the most natural explanation of the statement in the *Gwydir Memorials*, that Morgan "was
brought up in learning at Gwydir."   It is difficult
to see how he could otherwise have been educated.
Gwydir is more than ten miles from Ty Mawr, and
there were no schools of any kind near ; Llanrwst
Grammar School was not founded till after his
death.   Morgan's parents had no means of educat-
ing him, which is sufficiently attested by the fact
that he afterwards entered Cambridge as a sizar.
The Gwydir chaplain probably officiated minis-
terially sometimes at Penmachno church, Morgan
most likely attended the catechetical services, and
may have attracted the attention of the chaplain
as a promising lad, and so introduced to the
favourable notice of the Squire of Gwydir, where
he was afterwards taken in and educated.   The
chaplain's room, still existing, on the left-hand
side of the principal entrance to Gwydir, was the
school-room where Morgan was first taught his
Latin grammar.

Most of the present building of Gwydir was built early in the present century, though traces of the style of the sixteenth remain. Some of the rooms contain carved work of the time of Elizabeth and James I., and a screen is shown said to have been worked by Mary Queen of Scots.

CHAPTER II.

Religious State of Wales in Morgan's Early Days—First Book of Common Prayer—The " Use of Bangor "—Progress of the Reformation in Wales—The English Liturgy—Welsh Translation of the Epistles and Gospels—*Kynniver Llith a ban*—The Bishops of Wales and the Reformation — Welsh Martyrs — Exiles—William Salesbury.

DURING the short reigns of Edward and Mary there was a strong Anglican party, and a strong Romanist party, in the Church of England ; most Welsh people belonged to the latter. But the great body of the nation was more or less indifferent to the theological questions then at issue, otherwise the religious changes could not have been so easily effected.

Both Books of Common Prayer, of 1549 and 1552, retained Catholic doctrine and ritual as sanctioned by antiquity, omitting mediæval accretions. Before this a liturgy of various " Uses " existed in different dioceses. " And whereas heretofore there hath been great diversity in saying and singing in churches within this realm ; some following Salisbury Use, some Hereford Use, and some the Use of Bangor, some York, some Lincoln ; and from henceforth all the whole Realm shall have but one Use."[1] It is a mistake to suppose

---

[1] Preface to the Book of Common Prayer.

that while the Roman Catholic religion prevailed, there was perfect uniformity in public worship. These various "Uses" show that before the Book of Common Prayer, which is based mainly on the Use of Salisbury, was set forth, there was far less uniformity then than there is now.

There is a manuscript of the "Use of Bangor" in the Bangor Cathedral Library—a folio of moderate thickness, containing thirty-two Offices, with anthems and musical notes. At the beginning are the Offices for making and ordaining the Acolyti, Sub-diaconi, Diaconi, Presbyteri, Episcopi ; forms for consecrating churches and churchyards ; forms for the exorcising of bread, cheese, and honey ; Offices for all Sundays and holy days throughout the year ; prayers in times of pestilence, war, and other occasions. The thirteenth Office contains the mass; the nineteenth, Form of the Chapter electing their Bishop. In the latter end is the Office of Baptism (in which trine immersion is expressly enjoined) ; Communion, Visiting the Sick, Burying the Dead, &c. The rubric part is all red. Instead of pagination the folios are numbered from 1 to 33, at very irregular intervals. These are chapters or sections relating to various episcopal functions. It has an illumination, representing a Bishop with his crozier in the one hand, and the brush of sprinkling in the other, and is in the act of sprinkling holy water on the church which he is consecrating. He is attended by priests, one holding the holy-water vessel. The Use of Bangor dates from 1291, probably,—the date of the Synod of the clergy which Anian held at S. Mary's Church, Bangor—when this Use was probably adopted for

D

the diocese. The Offices are, of course, all in Latin, and after the doctrine, rites, and ceremonies of the Church of Rome.

Strype testifies to the tenacity with which the Welsh people clung to the Roman ritual.

"Anno 1550. As to the success of the Reformation, it went on but slowly in the parts farther distant from London. In Wales, the people ordinarily carried their beads about with them to Church, and used them in prayer. And even at the Church at Carmarthen, while the Bishop was at the Communion table bareheaded doing his devotions, the people kneeled there and knocked their breasts at the sight of the Communion, using the same ceremonies as they had used in times past before the Mass. They brought their corpses to be buried with songs and candles lighted up about them. And one Dr. Hughes, ministering the Communion in the Cathedral Church of S. David's, did, after the popish manner, break the host into three pieces, putting one of the parts into the cup, and giving a whole cake to communicants without breaking the same."[1]

The reluctance of the Welsh people, naturally conservative, to break off from old-established forms and religious usages may be well imagined. Some of the customs to which Strype refers still exist. When the Methodists first came into Wales in the last century, the peasantry expressed their horror of them and their opinions by crossing their foreheads, and continued to pay great veneration to a tale called "Breuddwyd Mair," or Mary's

[1] Strype's *Memorials*, vol. ii. p. 357 (Ed. 1822).

Dream.[1] Singing at funerals, with offerings, is still common, especially in North Wales.[2] The "Gwylnos," or Vigil with the Dead on the eve of burial, was common enough twenty or thirty years ago. It was also usual, in many places, on such occasions to place three lighted candles[3] on the coffin— emblematic of the Trinity. On the Sunday after the funeral, each relative of the deceased knelt on his grave, exclaiming " Nefoedd iddo" (" Heaven to him "), or " May he be in heaven." The souls of children dying before their parents were regarded by them as so many candles. to light them to Paradise.

Nothing beyond the efforts of William Salesbury was done during the reign of Edward VI. to establish the Reformation in Wales. In 1550, he published *A brief and plain Introduction, teaching how to pronounce the letters in the British tongue, now commonly called Welsh.* He also published in the same year, *Battery of the Pope's Bottereulx, commonly called the High Altar.* A Welsh translation of the Epistles and Gospels for the whole year, was published in 1551 under the title of *Kynniver llith a ban o'r Ysgrythyr lan ac a ddar-*

---

[1] *Trysorva*, vol. ii. p. 516.

[2] The " offrwm," or offering, at funerals is a remnant of the custom of saying masses for the dead. In some places it is the custom to announce the amount of the offerings at the close of the Burial Service, and the sum total is taken as the criterion of the extent of respect entertained for the deceased.

[3] I saw lately, in a Welsh farm-house, three candlesticks of solid brass, which had been in the family for a long time for that exclusive use, and left to the present owner as an heirloom.

lleir yr Eccleis pryd Commun, Y Sulieu, a'r Gwilieu trwy'r vlwyddyn. This was also the work of Salesbury, as well as a translation of the new Order of Communion Service, issued in 1548 by order of the King, in which " Sacrifice of the Mass " was changed into " Lord's Supper," and the cup restored to the laity.

The Welsh bishops did very little to help the work of the Reformation in Wales. Warton, Bishop of S. Asaph, was seldom in the cathedral city during the twenty years of his episcopate. He lived much at Denbigh and Wrexham, and kept so great and expensive an establishment that, in order to obtain money, he let out on long leases the lands belonging to his bishopric, to its great impoverishment. Bulkeley, Bishop of Bangor, in the reigns of Edward and Mary, sold the bells out of the cathedral tower at Bangor, with some articles of church furniture : mitres, copes, and chalices. But they were sold to pay off debts incurred by himself in " the defence of his poor church," to reclaim church property which had been taken in the time of his predecessor, and for the repairs of the cathedral. Bulkeley was the first bishop who had resided in the diocese of Bangor for upwards of one hundred years. Being a Welshman, he seems to have been in all respects a promoter of the good of his diocese. The non-residence of his predecessors shows that this anomaly was not confined to the post-Reformation bishops of Wales. Nor were they more avaricious and unprincipled, as is sometimes alleged. Kitchin of Llandaff ruined the See by leasing the estates for his own benefit. Himself a man of no principle, he adapted himself

to all the changes of the reigns of Henry, Edward,
Mary, and Elizabeth; and so held his bishopric for
twenty-one years undisturbed. In his oath to the
king, at his consecration on May 3, 1545, he professed to have had "the veil of darkness of the
usurped power, authority and jurisdiction of the
See and Bishop of Rome clearly taken away from
his eyes." But he allowed the same "veil of darkness" to be put on again in the reign of Mary.
His eyes, however, saw the light once more at the
accession of Elizabeth.

Mary, at her accession in 1553, determined to
restore the Roman ritual. Persecution followed.
Three Englishmen suffered martyrdom in Wales in
this reign. Robert Ferrar, Bishop of S. David's, was
burnt in the Market Place, Carmarthen, on Satur-
day, March 30, 1555, for allowing the marriage of
priests; denying the doctrine of Transubstantiation,
and affirming that man is justified by faith alone.
Rowlins White, a fisherman, was burnt at Cardiff
in the same year; and William Nichol suffered the
same death at Haverford West in 1558.

There were a few Welshmen who sympathized
with the reformers, Richard Davies, afterwards
successively Bishop of S. Asaph and S. David's,
being among the most prominent among them.
Edward VI. presented him to the Vicarage of
Burnham in 1550, with which he also held the
rectory of Maidsmoreton, Buckinghamshire; of
which preferments he was deprived in the time of
Mary. Davies fled to Geneva, where he suffered
much poverty; living, at first, on the alms and
contributions of his fellow-exiles. He soon became
so well acquainted with the French language that

he obtained a cure there, which afforded him a comfortable maintenance.

William Salesbury lived in hiding at Cae Du, Llansannan, Denbighshire, during the Marian persecutions. A chamber was curiously contrived for his concealment in this house, accessible by climbing inside the chimney. Such chimneys were very common in old Welsh houses. They were long and irregular, while the base was sufficiently roomy to accommodate a small family. Such was the chimney of Cae Du. Here among the Welsh hills, under the roof of the very house wherein he was born, Salesbury found a refuge during the reign of Mary.

CHAPTER III.

EARLY DAYS.

ELIZABETH, 1558—1603.

ARCHBISHOPS OF CANTERBURY.

MATTHEW PARKER, 1559—1575.
EDMUND GRINDAL, 1575—1583.
JOHN WHITGIFT, 1583—1604.

BISHOPS OF S. ASAPH.	*BISHOPS OF BANGOR.*
THOMAS GOLDWELL 1556—1560	WILLIAM GLYN, 1555—1559
RICHARD DAVIES, 1560—1561	ROWLAND MEYRICK, 1559—1566
THOMAS DAVIES, 1561—1573	NICHOLAS ROBINSON 1566—1586
WILLIAM HUGHES, 1573—1601	HUGH BELLOT, 1586—1596
WILLIAM MORGAN, 1601—1604	RICHARD VAUGHAN, 1596—1598
	HENRY ROWLANDS, 1598—1616

BISHOPS OF S. DAVID'S.	*BISHOPS OF LLANDAFF.*
HENRY MORGAN, 1554—1560	ANTHONY KITCHIN, 1545—1566
THOMAS YOUNG, 1560—1561	HUGH JONES, 1566—1575
RICHARD DAVIES, 1561—1582	WILLIAM BLETHIN, 1575—1591
MARMADUKE MIDDLETON, } 1582—1594	GERVASE BABING- TON, } 1591—1595
ANTHONY RUDD, 1594—1615	WILLIAM MORGAN, 1595—1601
	FRANCIS GODWIN, 1601—1618

Accession of Elizabeth—Her Caution—Revival of the Acts of
Supremacy and Uniformity—Escape of Goldwell—The Queen
and the Reformation—Numerical Strength of Anglicans and
Romanists—Consecration of Parker.

WILLIAM MORGAN was eleven years old when
Elizabeth ascended the throne. The first acts of

the Queen were conspicuous for the tact and shrewdness with which she ruled. She succeeded, for a time, in balancing the hopes and the fears of Romanists and Anglicans.

The exile reformers return safely, and the religious prisoners of the preceding reign are discharged. The petition in the Litany against " the tyranny of the Bishop of Rome and al hys detestable enormities," was suppressed. But it soon became evident that the royal trumpet was to give no uncertain sound. Parliament revived the Acts of Supremacy and Uniformity. Out of 9,400 beneficed clergy in England and Wales, 189 only refused to take the oath of the Royal supremacy; of whom 14 were bishops, and they were deprived. Kitchin of Llandaff submitted, and was allowed to retain his bishopric. Bishop Glyn, of Bangor, died about this time; while Goldwell of S. Asaph, and Morgan of S. David's refused to conform. Goldwell fled to Rome. Among the State (Domestic) Papers in the Public Record Office, are Particulars, dated 29 June, 1559, of his sudden departure. The Ports were ordered not to let him pass. The Bishop left because he owed the Queen £300, as appears from a letter, among the State Papers, sent by him to his brother Stephen. Goldwell managed to escape safely to Rome. The State Papers in the Record Office [1] contain some account of him when in Rome.

[1] State Papers (Domestic) Elizabeth, vol. xiv. 33, 41. Four discourses by Robert Barret, addressed probably to Walsyngham. The first dated 20 January, 1580-1, details the course of his travels for the six years preceding in Flanders, France, Italy, and Spain, and of the English persons with whom he came in contact. In Rome he was examined before Mr. Stukly. " One Mr. Shelly who calls himself Lorde

He sat at the Council of Trent in 1562; and, afterwards, going to Rome, was appointed by the Pope (Pius IV.) to baptize Jews, and ordain such Englishmen as fled there for their religion. He was living at Rheims in 1580, and died the following year in Rome.

The history of the Reformation is full of great inconsistencies. Within the short period between the death of Henry VIII. and the accession of Elizabeth, the public profession of religion was thrice changed. These changes could not have been so easily effected had the majority of the nation felt decidedly on either side. The people

---

Prior of Ingland, *and one owld man called Gowldewell, some tyme, as they saye, a byshope in the papisticall time in ingland*, before whom I was sharply examined."

S. P. D. vol. clxxviii. paper 46. "I John Neale pryest *ordryd by the old byshoppe Goldwell at Rome abowne fyve yere since*, came into England—and upon intelligence of the late Statute touchinge banyshment of preystes accordinge to the tenour thereof sought passage at Woodbrydge and Baudsey haven in Suffolk the iiij[th] v[th] vj[th] seventh and eyghth daye of this present Maye, and upon the eyghth day was stayde at Alderton."

Vol. clxxx. "Examination of Francis Edwards taken on his return from France, before Ralph Chauntler, Deputy to the Mayor of Chichester, and Francis Cox, Preacher Commissioners for the examination of passengers. July 7, 1585. Edwards said he was a native of Wrexham, had been beyond the seas four years. In answer how he had spent his time abroad, he said: "In Studye, and was maynteyned in the Sermynarye at Rhemes, *and that he had some Relyve of one Goldewell, late Byshop of Asaph now being dead*, and was made Pryest at Rheimes about Chrestmas last past by a Bysshoppe of Bryttayne Suffrycane to ye Cardinal Guyer. He sayd he meant to go to Wales among his friends."

were strongly attached to the Tudors, and felt proud of their lineage, notwithstanding their arbitrary sway. The despotism of Elizabeth was second only to that of her father. But in her case it may have been a result of, as well as a reaction from, the reign of Mary. There was now so much to build up, and reinstate, and so many enemies to encounter, that it required strength of will to guide into proper channels the conflicting religious opinions which had now come to the surface. If the Queen herself was haughty, she also, in her turn, had sometimes to listen to coarse, bitter, and cutting discourses. Mr. Dering, in his sermon, informed her majesty that "she began her reign with the meekness of a lamb, but that now she was an untamed heifer." An instance also of the unrestrained language indulged in by the Puritan party comes from the lips of one of the most eminent of that body, Thomas Cartwright, who spoke of the Bishop's spiritual courts as "damnable, devilish, and detestable."

In the absence of an official return showing the relative strength of the Anglican and Roman Communions at this time, there are no trustworthy statistics to prove which was the strongest. Lingard thinks that one-half the nation was Roman Catholic in the middle of the reign of Elizabeth. Hallam, on the other hand, says that two-thirds were Anglicans and one-third Romanists. Cardinal Bentivoglio reckons the zealous Roman Catholics of this period at one-thirtieth part of the nation: the number who were indifferent, at four-fifths of the nation; the proportion prepared to make any sacrifice on either side as very few indeed.[1]   The last seems the most correct estimate of the three, and is borne out by the fact that the public profession of religion was thrice changed in a short space of time with very little difficulty.

[1] *Burleigh and his Times* (Macaulay), p. 233.

CHAPTER IV.

CONSECRATION OF WELSH BISHOPS.—1559-60.

Consecrations of Rowland Meyrick — Richard Davies — Thomas Yonge—State of the Diocese of S. Asaph in 1560—Letter of Bishop Davies to Archbishop Parker—Effects of Confiscation—Translation of Davies to S. David's—S. Asaph Diocesan Council, 1561—The XXXVIII. Articles of Religion.

FOUR bishops, deprived in the time of Mary, officiated. at the consecration of Parker as Archbishop of Canterbury, Pole having died within a few hours of the death of the Queen. The service of Consecration took place, in due form, at Lambeth Palace Chapel, December 17, 1559. And on December 21st, in the same year, Parker consecrated Rowland Meyrick to Bangor, assisted by three English bishops, who had been exiles in the reign of Mary. On January 21, 1560, Richard Davies was consecrated to S. Asaph, and Thomas Yonge to S. David's. John Jewell was consecrated to Salisbury at the same time. " The worthiest divine," says Hooker, " Christendom hath bred for the space of some hundreds of years."

Bishop Davies, in the first year of his episcopate, made the following Return to Archbishop Parker of the state of the Diocese of S. Asaph at that time.

" Pleaseth it your Grace to be advertizede, that where you willed and required me, for certain considerations conducent to the general Reformation of the Clergie of the Province of Canterburie, to certifie your grace of this side of the fyrst Day of Februarie next, or so spedily as I might conveniently, of the names and surnames of all and singular Deanes, Archdeacons, Chaunclers, Chaunters, and others, having Dignitie in my Cathedrall Churche, with all Prebendaries of the same : And also of all and singular Parsones Vicars within my dioces, and how many of them, aswell of our Cathedral Church as of other beneficed in my dioces, be neither Prestes nor Deacons. Notinge also the names of all such as be learned and able to preache, and which of them be already lizensed do preach accordingly ; and fynallie howe many of them do keape hospitalitie.   So it is according unto my bowden dutie I made search through my Dioces for my diligent accomplishment of the same.   Wherein I have found as hereafter particularly ensueth." [1]

Here follows a list of the Cathedral and parochial clergy of the then eight Rural Deaneries of the diocese, all specifically named and described, with their degrees, &c. ; fourteen of whom were dignitaries. Thirteen, out of the hundred and thirty-four clergy in the diocese, are returned as non-resident. In this respect, the diocese did not suffer so much in Bishop Davies' time as it did later on. The Bishop complains that very few of his clergy had attained to evangelical truth ; the exceptions were : Hugh Evans, Dean of S. Asaph; John Price, Rector of Whittington, and Chancellor of the Cathedral ; Mr. Jenkins, Rector of Newtown ; Griffith Lloyd, Vicar of Llangwm, Dinmael.

The Bishop's complaint that so few of his clergy had attained to what he terms evangelical truth—

[1] Appendix LIX. : Browne Willis' *Survey of St. Asaph,* vol. ii. p. 136.

by which he meant the Reformation—shows how
tardy its progress was among the Welsh clergy as
well as the laity. The country had not recovered
itself from the violent convulsions of the two preceding reigns, and the confiscations of Henry, to
adapt itself to the new condition of things. The
Bishops were like shipwrecked mariners, endeavour-
ing to put together the shattered bulwarks of the
ship. The storm of confiscation had almost ruined
the parochial system and its revenues. Parker
issued an order in 1560, forbidding all his suffragans
to ordain mechanics, " many of whom by reason
either of their ignorance, or want of grave be-
haviour, rendered themselves despised, or hated by
the people." [1]

On the translation of Bishop Richard Davies to
S. David's, Thomas Davies succeeded to S. Asaph,
and began his episcopate vigorously, holding a
Diocesan Council, on Nov. 12, 1561, in furtherance
of the work of the Reformation. The resolutions
then agreed to, indicate that the removal of images
and relics had proceeded but very slowly indeed ;
and that due provision was about to be made for
public ministrations in the Welsh language, and
were as follow—

" That every of them shall forthwith avoyd, remove
and put away, or cause to be put away, all and every
fayned relyques and other superstycons had withyn ther
severall churches, and abolyshe ther aulters yn the same,
within eight days.

*   *   *   *   *   *

" The Litany to be sung or seyd on Wednesdays and
Frydays.

[1] Strype's *Parker*, Book II. chap. iv. p. 907.

"After the piystyll and gospell yn Englyshe, the same to be read also yn Welshe."

As the Bible and Book of Common Prayer had not yet been translated into Welsh, there could be no ministrations in that language according to the reformed liturgy. The Epistle and Gospel only were read in Welsh, from the *Kynniver Llith a Ban*, translated in 1551 by Salesbury. The Holy Communion Service, issued in 1548, appeared about the same time in Welsh, and was the only Office translated before the appearance of the first entire Welsh Prayer-Book in 1567,—intended to supersede the service of the Mass; but it was never, probably, adopted by the Welsh clergy. The Roman ritual continued in use among Welsh people for a much longer time than it did among the English. Its rejection was very gradual in Wales, and could not have been otherwise, because the people were not provided with a Bible and Liturgy in the vernacular for a long time after the people of England. Add to this that the majority of the Welsh clergy and laity evinced more affection for the old than the new ritual.

Among the prelates who subscribed to the XXXVIII. Articles of Religion of 1562, were Bishops Richard and Thomas Davies. The Articles put forward this year were reduced to thirty-eight by the omission of the twenty-ninth, the title of which was, "Impii non manducant Corpus Christi in usu cænæ," and the famous clause, "Habet ecclesia ritus Statuendi jus et in fidei controversis Auctoritatem," was added to the twentieth Article. The original document, containing the subscriptions, is now at Corpus Christi College, Cambridge.

CHAPTER V.

A.D. 1563.

Act of Parliament for Translating Bible and Prayer-Book into Welsh—Patent granted for printing them—The Welsh Bishops and the Translation—Salesbury appointed to the Work—At Abergwili—Correspondence with Parker.

IN the year 1563 Parliament passed an Act, which in its main provisions was as follows—

"Because the English tongue is not understanded of the most and greatest number of all her majesty's most loving and obedient subjects inhabiting within her Highness Dominion and Country of Wales,[1] being no small part of this realm, who therefore are utterly destitute of God's Holy Word, and do remain in the like or rather more darkness and ignorance than they were in the time of Papistry: Be it therefore enacted . . . That the Bishops of Hereford, Saint David's, Asaph, Bangor and Llandaff, and their successors, shall take such order amongst themselves for the soul's health of the Flocks committed to their charge within Wales. That the whole Bible containing the New Testament and the Old, with the Book of Common Prayer, and Administration of the Sacraments, as is now used within the Realm in English, to be truly and exactly translated into the British or

---

[1] This is evidence that the Welsh language was not on the point of extinction at the time of the Reformation. Its vitality called for this Act of Parliament.

Welsh tongue; (2) and that the same so translated being by them viewed, perused and allowed, be imprinted to such number at the least, that one of either sort may be had for every Cathedral, Collegiate and Parish Church, and Chapel of Ease, before the first Day of March, *Anno Dom.* One thousand five hundred sixty-six; (3) And that from that day forth, the whole Divine Service shall be used and said by the curates and ministers throughout all the said Dioceses where the Welsh tongue is commonly used, in the said British or Welsh tongue, such in manner and form as is now used in the English Tongue, and differing nothing in any Order or Form from the English Book; (4) For the which Books as imprinted the Parishoners of every of the said parishes shall pay the one Half or Moiety, and the Parson or Vicar of every of the said Parishes (where both be) or else the one of them where there is but one, shall pay the other half or moiety; (5) the Prices of which books shall be appointed and rated by the said Bishops or their successors, or by three of them at the least; (6) The which things if the said Bishops or their successors neglect to do, Then every one of them shall forfeit to the Queen's Majesty, her Heirs and Successors, the sum of forty pounds, to be levied on their goods and chattels.

"II. Be it further enacted by the Authority aforesaid, That every Minister and Curate within the Diocesses before said, where the Welsh Tongue is commonly used, shall from the Feast of Whitsuntide next ensuing until the aforesaid Day of March, which shall be in the year One thousand five hundred sixty-six, at all times of Communion declare and read the Gospel and Epistle of the Day in the Welsh Tongue,[1] to his or their parishoners in every of the said churches and chapels; and also once every week at the least, shall read or declare to their said

[1] This has reference, no doubt, to Salesbury's translation of them into Welsh in 1551.

E

Parishoners in the said Churches the Lord's Prayer, the Articles of the Christian Faith, the ten Commandments, and the Litany, as they are set forth in the English Tongue, in the said Welsh Tongue, with such other part of the Common Prayer and Divine Service as shall be appointed by the Bishop of the Diocess for the time being.

"III. And one Book containing the Bible, and one other Book of Common Prayer, in the English tongue, shall be bought and had in every Church throughout Wales in which the Bible and Book of Common Prayer in Welsh is to be had by force of this Act (if there be none already) before the first day of March, which shall be in the year of our Lord God, One thousand five hundred and sixty-six; (2) and the same books to remain in such convenient places within the said Churches, that such as understand them may resort at all convenient times to read and peruse the same: And also such as do not understand the said language, may, by conferring both Tongues together, the sooner come to the knowledge of the English Tongue; any Thing in this Act to the contrary notwithstanding." [1]

According to Strype, it was contemplated by this Statute that the Book of Homilies should also be translated into the Welsh language. But the Act contains no reference to it. The Queen granted a patent for seven years to William Salesbury, of Llanrwst, Gent: and to Thomas Waley of London, Printer, and to their heirs and assigns, with a Prohibition to all others, to print the translations so made; after they had been perused and allowed by the said Bishops, or any two of them. [2]

[1] Copied from Ruffhead's *Statutes at Large*, vol. ii. p. 568.
[2] Strype's *Annals of the Reformation* (1709), p. 391.

Scory, at this time Bishop of Hereford, did not, most likely, know Welsh : though Strype says he did. But Welsh was spoken in some parts of Herefordshire in the sixteenth century, and some of the churches contained Welsh Bibles which bore unmistakable marks of having been used. The " Use of Hereford," too, was the liturgy adopted in South Wales, and there was more intercourse between the clergy of South Wales and the diocese of Hereford, than between the North and South Wales clergy.

The only one of the four Welsh bishops who took any active part in the work of translating the Bible into Welsh was Richard Davies. It was not contemplated by the Act that the bishops should do the work themselves, but the responsibility was laid upon them ; and a penalty of £40, to be levied on each of them in default of the completion of the work in three years. The time granted was insufficient. The translators were engaged on what is known as Parker's Bible for a longer period, though the work was distributed fairly and equally among different hands. The Act made no provision for the cost of printing the Welsh Bible, though Parliament voted a thousand marks—nearly £700—towards the expense of publishing the English Bible. The imposing of a fine of £40 on each of the bishops was an additional hardship. No such penalty was imposed on the English bishops. Whether it was enforced or not, is not known ; but it is certain that the provisions of the Act, in other respects, were not carried out. It was difficult to find a competent Welsh scholar then, who could undertake the work of translation.

Among the bishops, Richard Davies was the only one equal to the task; and he was engaged on a portion of the English translation known as Parker's Bible. The translation of the Epistles and Gospels in 1551 marked Salesbury out for the work of Welsh translation, and which he undertook at the request of the Welsh bishops. So he tells us in his dedication of the completed translation of the New Testament.

"Whereas I, by our most vigilant Pastours, the Bishops of Wales, am called and substituted, though unworthy, somewhat to deale in perusing and setting forth of thys so worthy a matter."

To secure the help and counsel of Bishop Richard Davies, Salesbury resided at the Palace, Abergwili, for nearly two years. Writing to Parker, on the 19th March, 1565, Davies says—

"Pleaseth it your grace to be advertised that I received that piece of the Bible which your grace hath committed to me to be recognized, the fourth day of March last; and your Grace's letters dated the sixth of December, I received eight days before I received the portion of the Bible. I am in hand to perform your request, and will use as much diligence and speed as I can, having small help for that or for the Welsh Bible. Mr. Salisbury only taketh pain with me.

"For all such monuments as we had, Mr. Secretary hath them two years ago; some he had of Mr. Chanter, and some of me, which we had of our own store; but in the library of St. David's there is none at all. He had of me Giraldus Cambrensis, a Chronicle of England, the author unknown, and Galfridus Monemutensis. . . . One notable story

was in the Chronicle; how after the Saxons con-
quered, continual war remained betwixt the Britons
(then inhabitants of this realm) and the Saxons,
the Britons being Christians, and the Saxons
pagans. As occasion served they sometimes treated
of peace, and then met together, communed together,
and did eat and drink together. But after that
by the means of Austen the Saxons became
Christians in such sort as Austen had taught
them, the Britons would not after that neither
eat nor drink with them, nor yet salute them,
because they corrupted with superstition, images,
and idolatry, the true religion of Christ, which
the Britons had reserved pure among them from
the time of King Lucius." [1]

Writing to the Archbishop on the subject of the
English translation of the Bible, Davies in another
letter says—

"I am well forward in the recognising of that
part of the Bible that your grace hath committed
unto me. I will try by the help of God to finish it
with as much speed as I can. I bestow for the
performance of the same all such time as I can
spare from such affairs as will suffer no delays." [2]

The portions of "Parker's Bible" translated into
English by Bishop Davies were: the Books of
Joshua, Judges, Ruth, I. and II. Samuel. The
successor of Augustine enlisted and secured the
co-operation of a representative of the ancient
British Church, in the person of Richard Davies, to
translate the Scriptures into the English language.
The jealousy which at one time existed between

[1] Parker's *Correspondence*, p. 265.
[2] *Ibid.* p. 279.

Canterbury and the Welsh sees, and referred to by Bishop Davies in his letter to the Archbishop, did not exist in Parker's time. Nor has there been a revival of it since, but an ever-increasing desire to strengthen the union.

CHAPTER VI.

COLLEGE CAREER.

Morgan matriculates at Cambridge—Masters of S. John's College in his Time—Whitgift appointed Lady Margaret Professor of Divinity (1565)—Disturbance at S. John's College respecting Vestments—Controversy between Whitgift and Carter—Morgan graduates (1567-8) — The Tradition respecting the College Chaplaincy.

MORGAN matriculated at S. John's College, Cambridge, in 1564, when he was about seventeen years of age. The twelfth Master of the College, Richard Longeworth, had been appointed in the same year, and continued there beyond Morgan's undergraduate days, from 1564 to 1569. Students went to the Universities then when about thirteen or fourteen years old. Want of means and early training prevented Morgan from entering at an earlier age. He must have pursued his studies with a tenacity of purpose to be able to enter at all. There can be no doubt that the excellency of his general conduct, his talents and acquirements, secured for him the necessary help from Gwydir. Without this assistance it is difficult to see how any definite shape could have been given to his career. The " Catalogus Episcoporum," &c.,[1] has

---

[1] Baker's *Hist. S. John's Coll. Cambridge*, vol. i. p. 254.

the following entry : " Quo anno admissus fuerit in
Collegium non satis liquet, admissus vero fuit
sizator ex foundatione doctoris Dowman pro. Mro.
Dakyns socio Coll. Jun. 9, an. 1565 ;[1] admissus in
album sive matriculam acad. Joannensis et quad-
rantarius, Febr. 26, an. 1564."

Morgan, probably, secured this sizarship through
the influence of Canon John Wynne, then Rector
of Llanrhaiadr-yn-Kinmerch, a member of S. John's
College, and connected with the Gwydir family.
Whitgift became Lady Margaret Professor of
Divinity at Cambridge in 1565 ; Morgan, no doubt,
attended his lectures.   The University was, at this
time, in a state of agitation on the question of
vestments.   Informed that some statutes were in
preparation for the enforcement of uniformity of
vestments, particularly an injunction to wear surplices at the University, Whitgift promoted the
writing of a joint letter to Cecil from all the heads
of Colleges at Cambridge, earnestly desiring him
to prevent, if possible, the issue of such an injunction, as it would not be acceptable at the University.
This address gave such offence at Court, that
Whitgift had to apologize for the action he had
taken.   But he became of such high reputation at
Cambridge as a preacher, disciplinarian, and re-
storer of order there, that in 1566 the University
granted him a license, under their common seal, to
preach throughout the realm ; the salary of his
professorship was raised by the University, as a
testimony to his worth, from twenty marks to
twenty pounds.   Soon afterwards Whitgift became
Regius Professor of Divinity.

[1] Regr. Coll. Jo.

The disorder on the vestment question in 1565 appears to have been promoted by Fellows and scholars, "chiefly the younger sort." Morgan, as an undergraduate, was an eye-witness of the disturbance ; and, as a freshman, probably only a passive observer. As the incident is an epoch in the history of the College, and an event in Morgan's college career, the narrative of it [1] shall be introduced here.

" ' The College in great uproar. About the beginning of Dec. 1565, the fellows and scholars, chiefly the younger sort, to the number of near 300, some said, threw off the surplices with one consent. Longeworth the master being absent, the most part of the College Company came into the Chapel one Festival Day without their surplices and hoods . . . . and withal made some diversity in the manner of the administration of the Communion : and so continued to do : And this the said Master upon his return allowed, without complaint to any Magistrate, or endeavour to restore the former antient Usage.' Cecil wrote to the College (' many members whereof had humbly writ to him, that their consciences might not be forced to receive the ceremony they had laid aside ') charging them with ' vain-glory, and affectation of popularity, and contempt of laws.' To the V.C. he wrote, 10 Dec. 1565, saying that the Queen required the misdeameanour to be severely punished . . . . those who riotously railed against these orders, to be suspended from preaching . . . . Cecil sent for Longeworth, and compelled him, 14 Dec. to confess himself faulty in suffering the Fellows and scholars to continue in their innovations."

The famous controversy between Whitgift and

[1] *Hist. S. John's College, Cambridge,* vol. ii. p. 587.

Cartwright was at its height when Morgan went to Cambridge. The warm manner in which he speaks of Whitgift clearly indicates that Morgan's sympathies were with his tutor on the questions at issue.

Morgan took his degree of Bachelor of Arts in 1567 or 1568. "Artium bac. an. 1567-8. Incipit in Artibus (una cum Gul. Whitacre etc.) an. 1570-1;[1] designatus Joannensis in registro academiæ. (Muntias sector, quia nostrum esse valde velim.)"[2]

The tradition at Penmachno that Morgan continued at Cambridge for twelve or thirteen years as lecturer and chaplain to his college, is not corroborated by the *History of S. John's College*. There is no record of him after the year 1571, when he took his Master's degree.

S. John's College, Cambridge, appears to have been an attraction to Welshmen, before the foundation of Jesus College, Oxford, in 1573; and was probably regarded by them as a Welsh College, because it was founded by Margaret Tudor, mother of Henry VII. Bishops Morgan, Davies, Vaughan, Bellott; Dean Goodman, Archdeacon Prys, and Canon Wynne were all educated at this College.

[1] Regr. Acad.
[2] *Hist. S. John's College, Cambridge*, vol. i. p. 254.

CHAPTER VII.

A.D. 1567.

Publication of the first Welsh Translation of the New Testament and Book of Common Prayer—Salesbury's Scholarship—His Knowledge of Welsh — The Dispute between Davies and Salesbury.

IN the same year that Morgan took his degree were published the Welsh translation of the New Testament and of the Book of Common Prayer— the joint work of Bishop Richard Davies and William Salesbury, on which they had been engaged at Abergwili for upwards of three years. The New Testament was printed in black-letter, in a small quarto volume of 399 pages, and contained the same divisions into chapters as the present Welsh Testament, with arguments and contents to each book and chapter, and explanations of difficult words in the margin. The first Epistle to Timothy, the Epistle to the Hebrews, the Epistle of S. James, and the first and second Epistles of S. Peter— translated by Bishop Davies, and the Book of Revelation—translated by Precentor Huet, are divided into verses: the remainder, translated by Salesbury, does not contain the division into verses. This is a curious omission on the part of Salesbury.

It was not printed by John Waley, to whom the

patent was granted, but by Henry Denham, "at the costes and charges of Humphrey Toy."

Robert Toy, the father of Humphrey Toy, had carried on the business of a printer and publisher at the Bell, S. Paul's Churchyard, London, from 1541 to 1546, when he died. His widow, Mrs. Elizabeth Toy, was a Welshwoman, and is supposed to have influenced her son to undertake the publication of Salesbury's Testament.[1]   There was a Robert Toy, possibly another son, living at Carmarthen about this time, for he signed a petition, with Bishop Davies and others, to the Queen to found Carmarthen Grammar School in 1576. Robert Toy, probably at the request of the Bishop, helped on the publication of the work. "At the costes and charges of Humphrey Toy," was probably a compliment added to the title-page by the Bishop and Salesbury, in acknowledgment of their obligations to him for undertaking the work.

The translators did not confine themselves to one source, but followed partly the Greek Testament published by Stephanus (1551), with Erasmus' Latin translation, and they probably availed themselves of the help of the Geneva Bible of 1560, and of Beza's Latin translation which appeared in 1565.

Of Salesbury's scholarship there can be no doubt. Sir John Wyn testifies that he "was one of the profound scholars and skilful linguists" of his time, "and especially an hebrician, whereof there was not many in those days."[2]   He was quite as good a Greek scholar as Bishop Morgan, perhaps superior to him. The alteration of Salesbury's Version by

[1] Sir Samuel R. Meyrick's *Heraldry*, vol. i. p. 182.
[2] *Memoirs*, p. 94.

Morgan does not show original knowledge; but he relies largely on the Vulgate and Beza.

Bishop Davies and Precentor Huet were better conversant with the Welsh language than Salesbury was, notwithstanding that he undertook by far the greatest portion of the work of translation. Salesbury's experience is in accord with that of the present day, that a knowledge of Welsh cannot be acquired in after life to such perfection as that a person should be able to read, speak, and write with the power and effect peculiar to the home-born Welsh.

The defective Welsh of Salesbury's translation was a fatal hindrance to its popular use. The absence of the initial mutations reminds one much of the modern Anglicized Welshman, proving beyond all doubt that the translator had not been accustomed to the colloquial Welsh, which qualified Morgan to make a more readable and lasting translation. Salesbury's vocabulary was necessarily limited, the defect being frequently supplied by the introduction of purely English words, of which the following are examples: "Vy *monei* at y cyfnewidwyr" (Matt. xxv. 27); "Ac *mal* y *descendant* o'r mynyth" (Matt. xvii. 9); "Amprofitiol, amyn yr awrhon yn *profitiol* y ti ac i minheu" (Phil. 11).

Huet renders the oft-quoted verse, "Behold, I stand at the door and knock" (Rev. iii. 20) more forcibly than the present English and Welsh Versions do: " *Syna*, ydwyf yn sefyll wrth y drws, ac yn *taro*," "Be *astonished*, I stand at the door *and strike*."

Prefixed to this translation is a long and

interesting letter in the Welsh language written by Bishop Davies, addressed to the Welsh people, wherein he says—

"Look at the fashion of the world : there thou shalt have a temptation.   Such is the greediness of the world this day for land, gold, silver, and riches, that but few are to be found who trust in God and his promises.   By rapine and theft, perjury, deceit, falsehood, and arrogance, as with hooks, men of all sorts gather and draw to themselves.   God will not drown the world again with the waters of a deluge ; but lust for the things of this world has drowned Wales at this day, and has driven away everything good and virtuous.   For what is office in Wales in the present age but a hook, with which he who holds it draws to himself the fleece and the flesh of his neighbour?   What are learning, knowledge, and skill in the law, but thorns in the sides of neighbours, to cause them to stand aloof?   Often, in Wales, the hall of the gentleman is found to be the refuge of thieves . . . . Therefore I say that were it not for the arms and the wings of the gentry, there would be but little theft in Wales."

Simultaneously a Welsh translation of the Book of Common Prayer appeared, also printed "by Henry Denham, at the costes and charges of Humphrey Toy."

Bishop Davies and Salesbury were both engaged on a Welsh translation of the Old Testament, and had resided together at Abergwili for that purpose. According to Sir John Wyn, "they were very onward, and had gone through with it, if variance had not happened between them for the general sense and etymology of one word, which the Bishop would have to be one way, and William Salesbury another, to the great loss of the old British and mother tongue : for being together they drew Homilies, Books, and divers other Tracts in the British tongue, and had done far more if that unlucky division had not happened, for the Bishop lived five or six years after, and William Salesbury about twenty-four, but gave over writing, more was the pity."

What that unhappy word was we are not told. Salesbury's vow [1] that he would neither write nor speak a word in Welsh after this, indicates that the disputed word was a Welsh one. If so it will be readily granted that the Bishop was a higher authority than Salesbury on Welsh philology.

Speaking of Davies' Episcopate at S. David's, Sir John Wyn continues, " He governed like himself, and for the honour of our nation (loving entirely the North Wales men), whom he placed in great numbers there, having ever this saying in his mouth (" Myn y firi Faglog ") his familiar oath : " I will plant you North Wales men, grow if you list." . . . . . Oh ! how my heart doth warm by recording the memory of so worthy a man ! He dyed poor, having never had regard to riches," [2] at Abergwili on the 7th Novr. 1581, and was buried in the parish church of Abergwili.[3]

[1] *Enwogion y Ffydd*, vol. i. p. 64.
[2] *Memoirs*, p. 93.
[3] During the restoration of this church in 1850, the Bishop's grave was discovered, with his coffin and name on it. The grave was covered by an ordinary slab stone bearing the Bishop's name and the year of his death. The late Bishop Thirlwall, at his own expense, put up a mural marble monument in the chancel of the church, with a suitable inscription, near the Bishop's grave.

CHAPTER VIII.

The Church of Rome and the Reformation in Wales—The Pope denounces Reformation — *Yr Athrawiaeth Gristionogol* — *Y Drych Gristionogol*—Dr. Griffith Roberts and the Welsh Language—His Letter to the Welsh People—See of Bangor and Dr. Elis Price—See of Llandaff—Robinson of Bangor to Lord Burleigh.

POPE PIUS IV. sent his nuncio to England in 1560, with an offer to agree to all the changes made in the English Church and Liturgy, the translation of the Scriptures, and the appointment of Bishops, provided his supremacy were recognized. This letter, dated 5th May, 1560, is included in Dr. Cardwell's documentary *Annals of the Reformed Church of England*,[1] and is addressed by the Pope to the Queen in the following terms : " To our most dear daughter in Christ, Elizabeth, Queen of England." Pope Julius had, before this, in 1554, desired Cardinal Pole to absolve and reconcile bishops and priests made in Edward's reign, but did not direct their re-ordination. The Council of Trent, also, Session Nov. 30, 1562, decided by implication the validity of the English consecrations. The quasi sanction given to the English Liturgy by Pius IV. prevented an open separation

[1] Vol. i. p. 233. (Oxford 1839.)

between Anglican and Roman worshippers, according to the reformed ritual, in England, till the decree of Pius V., in 1569, denouncing the Reformation, and depriving the Queen of her crown.

Whatever may have been the effect of the Papal decree in England, the people of Wales had not up to this period experienced any perceptible change from the Roman to the Reformed ritual. The Welsh Book of Common Prayer of 1567 was not generally adopted for some time after this. Bishop Robinson of Bangor, in a letter to Sir William Cecil, dated 7th October, 1567,[1] writes: "Touching the Welsh peoples receaving of the Gospell, I find that ignorance contineweth many in the dreggs of superstition, which did grow chefly upon the blindness of the clergie, and also upon the closing of God's word from the people . . . . for the most part the priestes are too olde (they saye) to be put to schole. Upon this inabilitie to teache God's worde (for there are not six y^t can preache in yes three shierres). I have found since I came to this country images and aulters standing in churches undefaced, lewde and indecent vigils and watches observed, much pilgrimage goyng, many candles sett up to the honour of saintes, some reliques yet carried about, and all the countries full of bedes and knotts, besides other monuments of wilfull serving of God."

The Welsh members of the Anglican and Roman Communions were not indifferent at this time to the religious state of Wales from their own standpoint. Neither was the Welsh language undervalued by either, as a powerful medium of

_____
[1] State Paper Office : Dom. Eliz. 44, 27.

F

conveying religious instruction, and of influencing the Welsh masses generally.

Simultaneously with the publication of the Welsh New Testament and Prayer-Book in 1567, appeared a Welsh Catechism on "Christian Doctrine," or the *Athrawiaeth Gristionogol*,[1] by Morys Clynog, sometime Prebendary of York, and an officer in the Prerogative Court, under Cardinal Pole. On the death of Bishop Glyn, in 1558, Mary nominated Clynog to Bangor, but the Queen dying before his consecration, he, with Goldwell of S. Asaph, fled to Rome, and became the first rector of the English College, and was noted by the students there for his partiality to his countrymen of Wales, which gave rise to such friction between the resident English and Welsh students, that the Pope displaced Clynog from the Rectory in 1511.[2]

Deprived of his bishopric, Clynog sought to influence his countrymen through the Welsh press, by the publication of the *Athrawiaeth Gristionogol*. The following extracts show the nature of the work, and illustrate the author's style as a Welsh writer—

"Pumtheg dirgeledd yr Arg. Iesu Grist" (The Fifteen mysteries of the Lord Jesus Christ). "Y Pump lawenychus a ellir i myfyrio wrth fyned dros y paderau y waith gyntaf" (Five joys for meditation while going through the paternosters for the first time). "Y Pump dolur o'i 'styriaw wrth fyned Eilwaith dros y paderau" (The five wounds to be considered while going through the pater-

---

[1] The only existing copy of the original work is in the possession of Prince Lucien Bonaparte. A fac-simile reprint of it was published by the Cymmrodorion Society a few years ago.

[2] Wood's *Athen. Oxon.*

nosters a second time). "Gweddi 'r Arglwydd yn
yr ardd e' i scyrsio wrth y piler" (The Lord's
Prayer in the Garden, his scourging by the pillar).
"Esortiad i samio dy gydwybod" is rather a poor
rendering of "An exhortation to examine thy
conscience." But "Sacrafenau i santaidd fam
eglwys, y Bedydd a chrysma ne fedydd Escob" is
a truer rendering of "The Sacraments of the holy
mother Church, Baptism, the Chrysm, or Bishop's
Baptism,"—the Welsh term for Confirmation.

To this manual of devotion Dr. Griffith Roberts
of Milan wrote a Welsh preface: "Gruphydd fab
Rhobert yn annerch yr hyparch brelad, a'i dibal
gynheiliad M. Morys Clynoc: ac yn erchi iddo gan
duw, gynnyd gras a deduduch enaid a chorph."
"Griffith son of Robert saluting the venerable
prelate, and his never-failing patron, M. Morys
Clynoc ; and desiring him of God, increase of grace
and happiness in soul and body."

Of the early history of the learned and pious
author nothing is known further than that he was
educated at the University of Sienna, in Italy,
under the patronage of the Earl of Pembroke, from
which we may infer that he was a native of South
Wales. He settled at Milan, and became Canon
of the Cathedral, and Confessor to Cardinal Borromeo, Archbishop of Milan.[1] A man of great

[1] "From Lyons we went to Milan, where, in the palace of
Cardinal Borromeo, we found a Welshman lodged of the
name of Griffith Roberts—a man greatly respected there, and
Confessor to the said Cardinal—by whom we were very
socially welcomed and directed to the house of the English
priest in this city, of the name of Mr. Harries, who also gave
us a most kind reception." (*Harleian Miscellany*, vol. vii.
p. 132, col. 2.) Quoted in *Llyfr. y Cymry*, p. 22.

spirituality of mind and feeling, Dr. Roberts wrote a Welsh manual of devotion himself also, which he designated *Y Dryck Gristionogol,* or the "Christian Looking-Glass." Following the Preface is a note by Dr. Rhosier Smith, a native of S. Asaph, to this effect—

"Yr achos a'r modh y dodwyd y llyfr yma mywn Print, o waith yr athro mawr o Dhinas Fulan yngwlad yr Idal.

"O dref Roan

"Eych gwladwr caredig

"R. S."[1]

Amidst the grandeur of the historic and far-famed marble cathedral of Milan, and the honours conferred upon himself, Canon Roberts did not forget his native Wales, nor lose his affection for his mother tongue. He, although a stranger in a strange land, with Bishop Morgan in his own country, were the two greatest Welsh scholars, and representative Welshmen of the period. Far more deeply rooted in their large hearts than any sentimental patriotism, was the inborn, earnest desire for the spiritual welfare of their nation after the flesh. "I do not seek any repayment or thanks for my trouble and good wishes," writes the Canon in his Preface, "but to be a partaker of the prayers of every faithful Welshman, who may derive any

[1] "The cause and the means whereby this book was put in print, the work of the great teacher from the City of Milan in the country of Italy.

"From the town of Rouon

"Your loving countryman

"R. S."

consolation or good to his soul by the perusal or the hearing of the reading of this book."

The name of Dr. Griffith Roberts is pre-eminent as a Welsh grammarian, and the author of the first Welsh Grammar that was ever published. A work well known, no doubt, to Bishop Morgan, and helpful to him in the complicated and not yet settled question of Welsh orthography. "It seemed well to me," says Rhosier Smith, in his Welsh translation[1] of the Catechism of Petrius Cansius, "to follow the orthography of the venerable and excellent teacher, Dr. Griffith Roberts, Canon Theological of the Mother Church of the City of Milan, a man that deserves everlasting praise, not only for his many virtues, but also for his learning and knowledge, especially in the Welsh language."[2]

The task of writing a Welsh grammar could not have fallen into worthier hands. Indeed, it may be doubted whether there was, at this time, any other Welshman competent to undertake the work. It is a remarkable phenomenon in the history of Welsh literature, that the first grammar of the language should have issued from the pen of a Welshman in the cloisters of Milan Cathedral, and printed in that city, in 1567.

No one perusing the grammar, and the Doctor's preface to the *Drych Gristionogol,*—addressed to his " beloved Welshpeople, desiring their prosperity and success,"—can doubt his scholarship and patriotism. Independently of its literary excellencies, the letter is of historic interest, having

[1] Published in Paris in 1611.
[2] *Llyfr. y Cymry*, p. 86.

reference to the prestige of the Welsh people, their early Christianity, and their noble army of saints and martyrs. The entire absence of any reference to the work of the English Reformation is noticeable, and can be accounted for by the fact that no Papal decree had then been issued against it, and that the influence of the Roman Communion in Wales had not, at that time, been weakened to any great extent.

The Canon's description of the moral state of Wales—which he had probably heard from the lips of Morys Clynog, the exile Bishop-designate of Bangor—agrees with the words of Bishop Davies, in his preface to Salesbury's Welsh Testament, published in the same year.

"I hear," writes Roberts, "that there are many places in Wales, yea, whole counties without one Christian in them, most of them living like beasts, not knowing anything good, only that they retain in their memory the name of Christ, without knowing what Christ is more than beasts. And in those places where they are Christians, they are only those who are common and poor who follow Christ. The gentry and the wealthy are without thought of faith in the world, neither hot nor cold : So (Christ says) *I will spue thee out of my mouth,* as it is natural for a man to spue lukewarm water from his mouth. But in England the gentry are often good and show a good example in life and faith : the Welsh gentry give example to the poor and common people to be without any faith or conscience. Therefore they will have to render an account in the day of reckoning, not only for their own shortcomings, but for their want of good example.

*   *   *   *   *   *

"God and Mary be with you all, and grant us to live in the fold of Christ, so that we may all meet together in the heavenly Paradise, and reign with God for ever.

"From Milan,

"Yours,

"G. R."

This testimony is true. Instances upon instances could be adduced in corroboration of it. Let one out of many suffice, as illustrating the worldly, grasping spirit of the age. An attempt was made to foist the notorious Dr. Elis Price into the see of Bangor, at the recommendation of the Earl of Pembroke. Price was not even in Orders, "a creature of the Earl of Leicester, and devoted to all his bad designs."[1] A tyrant, and the terror of his subordinates,[2] but cringing to those in authority. How such a man could be recommended for a bishopric is inconceivable, devoid as he was of even the semblance of religion. Parker successfully opposed the appointment. Huet, the coadjutor of Davies and Salesbury in the work of translating the Welsh Testament, had been recommended to Parker for a bishopric, as appears from the letter of the Archbishop to Cecil, dated 7th Feb. 1565, in which he also refers to "Dr. Ellis Price having been

[1] Williams' *Eminent Welshmen.*

[2] A servant of Price was killed by mistake for his master, during an election disturbance at Denbigh, in 1553, when Sir John Salesbury, of Lleweni, was returned to Parliament for the county. An ill-feeling had existed before between the criminals and Dr. Price. George Salesbury, John Vane Salesbury, Richard Salesbury, and others named Pigot and Knowsley were tried before Chief Justice Bromley, at Shrewsbury summer assizes. Richard Salesbury, Pigot, and Knowsley were sentenced to death, and executed at Denbigh.

aforetimes sheriff of the shire, neither being priest or having any priestly disposition. I had rather for my part dissent from my Lord of Pembroke's request, than to commend a doubtful man to the Queen's highness, as yet persuaded, I would be loth to lay my hands on."[1]

A resolution was taken to supply the two vacant sees of Llandaff and Bangor, in Feb. 1565, the former having been in effect void for three years, and required a vigilant bishop; but the great dilapidations had so impoverished the see that few were prepared to accept it. The diocese of Bangor was also much out of order; there being no preaching, and pensionary concubinage openly continued, which was an allowance of concubines to the clergy by paying a pension, notwithstanding the liberty of marriage was granted. In the diocese of S. David's also concubinage was openly permitted, upon a payment of tribute to the priest's superior. This arrangement, says Strype, was regarded by the public as affording some protection to their wives and daughters.[2]

---

[1] *Parker Correspondence*, p. 257.

[2] At the sessions for Carnarvonshire, held at Carnarvon after the Feast of the Conception, in 1499, the matter was before the Court; and the record recites that "many and divers vicious priests and clerks within holy orders, within the Principality of North Wales, defile many women, wives and daughters of the Prince's tenants." The law then punished the husbands and fathers, and not the offending priests. It was decided at that court, however, that in future the priests or clerks "so unvirtuously disposed" should be distrained of their goods and lands, and for want of sufficient distress should be imprisoned until satisfaction had been given (*Records of Carnarvon*, p. 297, quoted in *Civil War in Wales and the Marches*, vol. i. p. 7).

Nicholas Robinson was appointed to Bangor, and Hugh Jones to Llandaff; the first Welshman, says Godwin, who presided over this see for three hundred years. The other Welsh sees were also occupied, for the most part, by Englishmen during the middle ages—the appointments being dictated by political motives. The first Welshman who had for a long time occupied a Welsh bishopric was appointed by Henry VIII., in 1542, to Bangor, in the person of Arthur Bulkeley.

PART II.—1567 TO 1595.

CHAPTER IX.

Date of Morgan's Ordination—Morgan's Acquaintance with Bishop William Hughes at Cambridge—Morgan's Title to Holy Orders —Founding of Jesus College, Oxford—Morgan Vicar of Welshpool—The Need of a Welsh Bible—John Penry on Welsh Reading—Morgan as a Welsh Reader and Preacher—Morgan's Marriage—Whitgift Vice-President of the Marches—His "Memorandum" to the Privy Council on the Religious State of Wales—Whitgift applies for a Special Commission for Wales— A Romish Recusant.

THERE is no record whatever of Morgan's ordination as deacon and priest. He took his degree of B.A. in 1567, three years before he was eligible to take Holy Orders, if we accept the year 1547 as the correct date of his birth. In the absence of any record it is impossible to say where these years were spent; possibly, at Cambridge. He took his degree of M.A. in 1571,[1] when he was between twenty-three and four years of age, and he may have taken Holy Orders in the same year. It is certain that he was in priest's orders in 1575; for he was instituted to the Vicarage of Welshpool on the 8th August in that year. Doctor Gwyn, by will dated 1571, founded three Fellow-

[1] *Regr. Acad. Cantabr.*

ships in S. John's College, Cambridge, tenable by natives of the parishes of Llanfair and Llanrhaiadr-yn-Kimerch; or in default, by such as should be born within the Commotts of Nant Conway and Maenan. Born in the former of these two Commotts, Morgan would be eligible to hold one of the Fellowships. I find no record in the *History of S. John's College* that he ever held such a position there, though these Fellowships are noted. The chaplaincy of his College, which he is supposed to have held, as already stated, but of which there is no record in the annals of the College, might have been his title to Holy Orders; still better the Fellowship—if he ever held one. If so, his ordination would have been at the hands of the Bishop of Ely; but there is no record of it among the diocesan papers there. Whether Morgan held a cure of souls in S. Asaph diocese before his promotion to Welshpool, it is impossible to say. The Diocesan Registry at S. Asaph was burnt down in 1688, and it now contains no documents anterior to that date.

Tradition has it that Dr. William Hughes—at this time Bishop of the diocese—himself a Cambridge man—met Morgan at the University, and was so impressed with his scholarship that he urged him to undertake the work of translating the Bible into Welsh, and inspired him with the idea which he afterwards so well carried out. If this tradition be true, it corroborates the other that Morgan remained at Cambridge after taking his degree, with the object, probably, of studying Hebrew.

Dr. Hughes took his degree of D.D. in 1570,[1]

---

[1] *Hist. Dio. St. Asaph* (Thomas), p. 226.

and probably remained at Cambridge from that year to 1573, when he became Bishop of S. Asaph. That he was at Cambridge, other than as an undergraduate, appears from a document at the British Museum, and printed in the *Archæologia Cambrensis*, entitled "A Discouerie of the present estate of the Bishopprick of S. Asaph. Doctor Hughes of Cātbr (Canterbury) first, and afterwards wēt to Cambridge."

From first to last Bishop Hughes continued to be the friend and patron of Morgan. The preferments he received up to his elevation to the episcopate, were entirely at the hands of that Bishop. All things considered, and in the absence of any record at Cambridge, or at the Diocesan Registry of Ely, that Morgan took Orders in that diocese, I am inclined to believe that he was ordained in 1573 as chaplain to Bishop Hughes; and that they both left the University for S. Asaph about the same time.

In the same year Jesus College, Oxford, was founded as essentially a Welsh college by Hugh Price, D.C.L., a native of Brecon, who had himself been educated at Oxford. Dr. Price petitioned Elizabeth to found a College on which he might bestow some property as an endowment, and a charter of foundation was granted June 27, 1573 ; by which it was prescribed that the College should be erected by the name of "Jesus College, within the city and University of Oxford, of Queen Elizabeth's foundation." Dr. Price settled some estates in Breconshire of the annual value of £160, to support the institution ; and bequeathed upwards of £1500 for the erection of the College buildings, towards which the Queen also gave a quantity of timber from the forests of Shotover and Stour.

Dr. Hugh Price had been constituted one of the first prebendaries of Rochester about the year 1542, and likewise treasurer of S. David's.[1] It was just a year before his death that he propounded the scheme of founding the College, which should extend the benefits of learning to Welshmen—a privilege not theretofore provided at Oxford.

The first discoverable notification of Morgan having entered the ministry, is that of his appointment to the Vicarage of Welshpool; but there is nothing left to show that he was ever resident there. The parish registers date no further than the year 1634.

Morgan was, doubtless, practically impressed with a necessity of a Welsh translation of the Bible, when he took charge of the parish of Welshpool. Three hundred years ago, that parish was more bi-lingual than it is now. Situate on the borders of England, the English element predominates, though some little Welsh is still spoken there. Morgan's Welsh-speaking parishioners, in common with others, were obliged to be satisfied with one lesson only from the New Testament, read from Salesbury's Welsh translation, the ruggedness of which must have grated on the ears of so accomplished a Welsh scholar as Vicar Morgan, when read aloud in church.

Speaking of the Welsh reading of the times, John Penry says:[2] "The second lesson was most evil read of the reader, and not understood of one

---

[1] Williams' *Dictionary of Eminent Welshmen*, p. 415.
[2] *Exhortation*, p. 11.

among ten of the hearers. Our ministers, though never so ignorant, yet all understanding English, might easily remedy this by conferring the English with the Welsh translation; and so where they understand not their own tongue, the English might direct them, and they their hearers. But they are far from taking this small pains. I would some of them in twenty years had learned to read Welsh at first sight."

Whether Penry ever knew or heard Morgan in his public ministrations it is, of course, impossible to say. But it is certain that he is not to be classified among those who, at this time, "could not read Welsh at first sight." Penry's condemnation of the Welsh reading of the clergy of the period may, however, be taken with some reservation, because Salesbury's translation, from which the second lesson was read, is so awkward and stiff, so regardless of the mutations, and antiquated in its style, that it was impossible for a superior Welsh scholar even, to read as correctly and intelligently as he might have done from a smoother and more readable translation. Speaking generally, the Welsh ministrations of the Church in Wales at this time were not efficient; *if*, as Penry says, those ministering at her altars were incapable of reading a chapter with intelligence. "Why," he asks, "cannot we have preaching in our own tongue?" "Because," he replies, "the minister is not able to utter his mind in Welsh."[1] But this inability of the Welsh clergy so to utter their minds was probably due more to the fact that the benefices were occupied by monoglot

[1] *Exhortation*, p. 11.

Englishmen, rather than to the incompetency of such Welsh clergy as there were to speak in their native tongue. We find that Bishop Hughes of S. Asaph refused to institute one Mr. Bagshaw to the living of Whittington in 1585, on the plea that he did not understand Welsh sufficiently well to minister therein to the parishioners.

Morgan was probably married after he went to Welshpool. His wife was Katharen, daughter of Grono ap Richard, and the widow of William ap dol Lloyd of Llanfair-dol-hayrn (Llanfair-tal-haiarn). She was descended from an old Oswestry family, and he probably met her at Oswestry, where she resided during her widowhood. According to the pedigree in Randle Holmes' volume in the British Museum, there was no issue of the marriage. The Evan Morgan who was at S. Asaph at the time of the Bishop's death, and who was also one of the Commissioners appointed by the Crown to inquire into the Bishop's affairs, was not a son, but a nephew—the son of a brother by his first wife. Randle Holmes gives the name in the pedigree as Ieuan ap Morgan.

In the year 1577, Whitgift, then Bishop of Worcester, was appointed Vice-President of the Marches of Wales, in the absence of Sir Henry Sydney, the President lately made Lord-Lieutenant of Ireland. Whitgift discharged his duties in this position with such ability and judgment, that he received from the Lords of the Privy Council their written thanks.[1]

Bishop Robinson of Bangor, in his Return to the Vice-President of the Council, dated Novr. 3, 1577

[1] Strype's *Life of Whitgift* (Ed. 1718), p. 82.

writes that there were " no recusants in his diocese, except one old priest named Barker, a very poor man." [1]

The following " Memorandum " by Whitgift to the Privy Council is interesting—

"At Eyton. January 15, 1578. Memorandum. That Thomas Laurence, Head master of Salop, and Richard Atkys, a third schoolmaster there, came before me George Bromley, (a lawyer, and one of the Council, as it seems, for those Marches), and uttered their knowledge concerning certain disorders committed in the House of John Edwards, of Thirsk (Chirk) in the County of Denbigh, and elsewhere by him, and others resorting to his house. In short, the sum of the articles were, " That Lady Throgmorton, wife of Mr. Justice Throgmorton, and others heard Mass in that house. That those that said Mass were five, and so apparelled that they could not be known. That one Hughes was the chief sayer of Mass : and that he came from beyond seas: that he taught the son of Sir John Throgmorton : that these Priests delivered to them that heard Mass, certain Beads, called Pardon Beads, which were little beads of glass ; and which they used to tie at the end of their other. And also another monument, which they called Agnus Dei. And that they ministered a corporal oath to such as they could draw to their Religion, and hearing of their Mass. That they Christened Children anew ; and swore their Parents that they should not come to Church. That they buried children and other Persons by night, because they would not admit, nor receive the Service now used. That upon S. Winifred's Day, Mrs. Edwards went to Halliwell (Holywell) by night, and there heard Mass in the night Season. That they carried thither

[1] State Papers (Domestic) in Record Office, vol. xiii. A.D. 1547—1580.

with them by night, in mails and cloak bags, all things pertaining to the saying of Mass. And that these Mass-Sayers used their Audience to receive Holy Water, and come to Confession."[1] ◆

Strype[2] tells us that these parts held so tenaciously to the Roman Ritual, that Whitgift, as Vice-President, applied for a Special Commission to him and some Welsh Bishops to deal with the matter; which was granted by a document dated Feb. 17, 1578, signed by Burleigh, Walsingham, and five other Privy Councillors, in pursuance of which Edwards was brought before Whitgift, and the Bishops of S. Asaph (William Hughes) and Bangor (Nicholas Robinson), to answer to the charges; but refused to give any reason for his action, promising that his wife, children and servants (who had concealed themselves) should appear before the Council. This was reported by the Vice-President to the Privy Council, when an order was issued in April, that Edwards should be kept in close imprisonment, and that steps should be taken to discover his wife and the rest.

The Order appears to have had the desired effect on the diocese generally, for Bishop Hughes, on November 3rd, wrote to the Vice-President, "no persons in his diocese refusing or neglecting to come to Church."[3]

[1] Strype's *Life of Whitgift* (Ed. 1718), p. 82.
[2] *Ibid*.
[3] State Papers (Domestic) in Record Office, vol. xiii. 1547 —1580, p. 564.

CHAPTER X.

A.D. 1578—1588.

Morgan promoted to Llanrhaiadr Vicarage—Takes the Degree of
B.D.—Of Retired Habits—Charges laid against him before the
Primate—Summoned to Lambeth—Good Results—Takes the
Degree of D.D.—A Local Tradition—The Court of High
Commission.

IN the year 1578 Bishop Hughes preferred Morgan
to the Vicarage of Llanrhaiadr-yn-mochnant,[1] in
succession to Peter ap David ap Rhys, who had
been Vicar since 1560.

A rural parish afforded more leisure for literary
work than a town parish; and Morgan's promotion
to Llanrhaiadr was, probably, not unconnected
with the work of translating the Bible. Since the
dispute between Bishop Davies and Salesbury, no
one had taken the work in hand; and it does not
appear that Morgan was authorized to undertake
it by the four Welsh Bishops, as Salesbury had
been. But it is certain that Bishops Hughes of
S. Asaph and Bellot of Bangor did encourage
Morgan to go on with it, by the loan of books; no
small boon in those days. Bishop Davies appears

[1] The meaning of the name is "The Church near the
Waterfall in the commot of Mochnant"—i.e. the rapid
Stream.

to have dropped the matter altogether; while Bishop Blethin of Llandaff does not seem to have interested himself at all in the matter. The work fell to the lot of the young Vicar of Llanrhaiadr, and he was well supported by his own Bishop.

Morgan took his degree of Bachelor of Divinity in the same year that he went to Llanrhaiadr: "Theo. bac. 1578; prædicator emissus ab academia eodem anno,"[1] i. e. The University sent him forth as a preacher in the same year.[2] This distinction, as in the case of Whitgift in 1565, shows that he was held in high reputation at the University.[3]

Having returned from the University, he settled down in the Vicarage house of the secluded parish of Llanrhaiadr, proceeding quietly with the work of translating the Old Testament.

A man of retired habits, he spent most of his time in his study. The parishioners, led by the Morrises of Henfachau, strong Romanists, laid charges against him before Whitgift; one of the complaints being that: he neglected parochial visiting, while so closely engaged on the work of translation; an allegation based on prejudice

[1] *Hist. S. John's Coll. Cambridge,* vol. i. p. 254.

[2] University preachers were first appointed by Pope Alexander VI., in 1502. The privilege of their appointment by the University was confirmed by Queen Elizabeth in 1561. Twelve graduates might be so appointed annually to preach in England and Ireland: "Licentia ordinariorum minime requisita."

[3] The fact that Dr. Morgan was appointed University preacher goes far to prove that he possessed some qualifications of an effective preacher. We have no contemporary testimony respecting his preaching powers, beyond the praises of two contemporary Welsh poets, who sang, in two poems, to his praise (see chap. xiv.).

against the man and his work. Morgan had undertaken a work destined to carry spiritual life and
light into every parish and hamlet in Wales, and
wherever the Welsh language is spoken ; so that
he might have claimed, in this respect, the whole
principality as his parish, just as Wesley claimed
the whole world as his parish.

There is also a hint that the indictment against
the Vicar contained some charge of a domestic
nature. Sir John Wyn, in his correspondence
respecting the tithes of Llanrwst, refers to his
certificate as having cleared up what was "objected
against him and his wife." The objections are not
specified, and they were probably as groundless as
the allegation of his incompetency to translate the
Bible.

It does not appear that any complaint was
made, in the first instance, to the Vicar's own
Diocesan ; though Rowlands, in *Llyfryddiaeth y
Cymry* (p. 43), says it was so ; but gives no
authority for the statement. Under ordinary
circumstances, this would have been the proper
and probable course. But knowing that there
existed a friendship between their Vicar and his
Bishop, and that he was brought to the diocese for
the very purpose of doing the translation which
they complained he was incapable of accom-
plishing, his parishioners would hesitate to complain
in that quarter. If such a complaint was made,
the Bishop would at once dismiss it, knowing
Morgan's qualifications for the task entrusted to
him. But the determined nature of the opposition
is evident from the fact that complaint was made
to the Archbishop of the Province.

The Vicar repaired to Lambeth to answer to the charges. This was not his first acquaintance with Whitgift, for he had attended his lectures at Cambridge; and he probably carried with him letters of commendation to the Archbishop from his own Diocesan. Morgan had by this time, as appears from a remark in the dedication, completed the translation of the Pentateuch, the manuscript of which, most likely, he took with him to Lambeth, as the most effectual answer to the charge of incompetency. Dean Goodman—an intimate friend of Whitgift, with whom, as member of the High Court of Commission, he was frequently brought into close contact—a Welsh scholar, was, in all probability, requested to look over the manuscript.

The Primate asked Morgan: "Are you as conversant with the Welsh language as you are with the Hebrew and the Greek?" "I hope, my Lord Archbishop," was the characteristic reply, "that you will allow me to assure your Grace that I understand my mother-tongue better than any other language."[1]

As Vice-President of the Lords Marches of Wales, Whitgift was frequently brought face to face with the Welsh difficulty, and was naturally desirous to know the extent to which the Welsh language was spoken and read. Hence the question he put to Morgan. The Archbishop may have had in his mind also the defective translation of Salesbury. Dean Goodman had, probably, pointed out to the Primate the necessity of a more readable Welsh New Testament.

. The Welsh Vicar made so great an impression

[1] *Llyfr. y Cymry*, p. 43.

on the Primate that he appointed him his chaplain, and encouraged him in every way to proceed with the work of translation. Had it not been for this timely help, the cost of printing would have deterred Morgan from proceeding further than the Pentateuch. So he tells us in the Dedication. His ill-disposed parishioners, unwittingly, led him to receive the help he so much needed, and the mischief they had planned became to him a stepping-stone to promotion. Morgan returned from Lambeth to Llanrhaiadr convinced of the truth: "As the bird by wandering, as the swallow by flying, so the curse causeless shall not come." [1]

The parish church of Llanrhaiadr is dedicated to S. Dogfan, and consists of one long nave, with tower, and principal entrance at the west end, and two chancel aisles of three bays; that on the south nearly coeval with the nave, that on the north earlier perhaps. No part of the church plate or furniture date as far back as the time of Vicar Morgan; neither do the parish registers go beyond the 4th July, 1677. The church is, as to its general features, much the same as it was three hundred years ago.

The present vicarage-house is the same house as Vicar Morgan—or rather Dr. Morgan, as he was known in his own parish and in Wales after the year 1583—lived in, with some later additions. During the last alteration a door-way, and two window-frames on each side of it, were brought to light in the north wall of the dining-room—which was built of wicker-work and clay; so that this must have been the front entrance in his time.

[1] Proverbs xxvi. 3.

A tradition exists in the parish that Morgan did most of the work of translation in a small wooden summer-house which he had erected for himself above the Mochnant—the stream which divides here the counties of Montgomery and Denbigh—distant about three hundred yards from the vicarage-house, above the parish church, and known to this day as " Pen-y-walk," where he spent much of his time reading.

In the same year—1583—that Morgan took his degree of D.D. at Cambridge, Whitgift was made Archbishop of Canterbury, and the High Court of Commission instituted, for enforcing the Acts of Supremacy and Uniformity, and which played so prominent a part in the history of the Church of England. Whitgift, who was at the head of the Commission, was a truly great man, and the undaunted champion of the rites, discipline, and revenues of the Church. The greatest part of his active life was devoted to her service; and her establishment, under God, to this day may be in a great measure attributed to his zeal and abilities. He had not the mildness and deep learning of an Usher, nor the spirituality and ascetic turn of a Leighton, who held the same rank in the Church; but he seemed to be an instrument raised up to preserve its ecclesiastical state, which enters so deeply into our whole political constitution that it would be difficult to dissociate one from the other.

CHAPTER XI.

A.D. 1586.

A Second Edition of the Welsh Prayer-Book—Archdeacon Prys
visits Morgan—Cynwal's Lines—Welsh Prayer-Book a Translation of the English — But differing in some Respects — Y
Nadolig — Yr Ystwyll—Y Garawys—Y Croglith — Y Pasc —
Offeiriad.

THE first Welsh Prayer-Book, which continued
in use nineteen years, clashed with the dialects of
North and South Wales. A new edition appeared
in 1586, containing "An Explanation of certain
wordes, being quarrelled withall, by some, for that
in this translation they be otherwise written, then
either the unlettered people, or some parts *of the
countrie sounde or speake them.*"

There is a perfect copy of the 1586 edition in
the S. Asaph Cathedral Library, and an imperfect
copy in the British Museum. It differs from the
first, in having illustrations, with suitable stanzas
in the Calendar, at the head of each month; and
from subsequent editions as wanting the Ordinal
and the XXXIX. Articles, which were translated
afterwards by Dr. John Davies, of Mallwyd.

Like the edition of 1576, it has been attributed
to Salesbury, because they are both after his
awkward style. The superior translation, however,
of some portions, indicates that it was not alto-

gether the work of one man ; as, for instance, the
Te Deum and *Magnificat*, so beautifully rendered,
probably, by the eminent Welsh poet, Archdeacon
Prys. Morgan was probably consulted in the
matter, and may have contributed some portion
of the translation. There is no authority for
attributing the whole work to any one man. As
parish priests, Morgan and Prys felt the need of a
better translation, and its publication could not
have failed to engage their attention.[1]

The title-page of each edition is a literal translation of the English Prayer-Book of 1552. "Rites "
is translated "cyneddfau," and not "deddfau," as
in the present edition. "Matins" = "Plygain,"
from pulli-cantus, probably, plu-ganu or the cock-
crowing. "Evensong" (so called because the
Evening Service was formerly sung) = "Gosper,"
from the Latin "Vesper." This is the colloquial
term in Welsh for the Evening Service.

Having the authority of a special Act of Parliament, the Welsh edition of 1567 of the Prayer-
Book, though a translation only, is of equal
authority, in law, with the original, and is the
standard as regards Welsh services. There is not,
so far as I know, any sealed copy of it. But it is
not, in all respects, a literal translation of the
English ; and there are instances of the introduction

---

[1] Prys used to visit Morgan at Llanrhaiadr. On one
occasion Cynwal, the poet of Penmachno, called at the
Vicarage when the Archdeacon was there, and addressed to
his rival the following stanza—

"Pa ryfedd bob wedd, heb i bant-fod, ar
    Hen fyd heb lifeiriant ;
  Ddfod afon eigion nant,
  Machno i Raidr Mochnant."

of English words, to supply the defective vocabulary of the translator, more particularly in the designation of some of the Offices; as, for instance, "Y Drefn am *Visitation* y Claf"; "Ffurf *Solemnization* neu drefnit Priodas"; "Bedydd *Public*"; "Bedydd *Preifat*."[1]

[1] Mr. Egerton Phillimore, M.A., lately published the commencement of the old Welsh Plygain Service (which breaks off quite abruptly), MS. in the Earl of Macclesfield's collection, a large folio volume between 1540 and 1560 by Ieuan ap William ap Dafydd ap Einws, Constable of Ruabon in 1554. Among its most important contents are a life of S. Collen, and the so-called hymns of S. Curig, differing widely from the printed texts. Another tract contained in it (written in April, 1545), contains some interesting memoranda in connection with the Reformation—about the taking of the chalice (Karregle) out of the churches in the writer's district, and others about the rentals of Cristionydd and the prices of corn. The Plygain Services occupy several pages of the MS. The following is a copy of the transcript. The reader that is familiar with the Welsh Prayer-Book cannot fail to discover that some of its sentences are embodied in our present Prayer-Book.

"Llyma ddechre y plygen y gwasaneth a ddwedir or bore hyd haner dydd.

"Avi Maria grasia blnia dominws digwm benedigta tuw yn muw lei erbws ieth benedigtws ffrwgtws y vendrus tuwei Jessus Krystws. Amen.

"Hyn a ddywedir yn gynta kyn dechre y plygen.

"Arglwydd, Egor vyngenef am gwevvsav i vynaic dy voliant i duw ystyria yn gymhorthwy ym arglwyd brysia un kymorth. Gogoniant i'r tad ae ir mab ac ir yspryd glan. Megis yr oedd yn y dechre ac y mae yn yr awr hon yn wastad ac yn oes oesoedd amen. Henffych gwêll vair gyflawn wyt o rad duw gida thydi y mae yn harglwydd ni ddyrchevwch ac ymdyrch avwn ni wrth yn harglwydd ni Iessu Grist. Kanwn i dduw voliant yn iachawdyr ni ac achyfwn i Lwyneb ef trwy gyffesv a chanwn Lsalymae ef i ddaw amen.

"Avi Maria grasia arglwydd mawr yw duw a brenin ar yr holl duwiav gana wrthy_l_ad yr arglwyd i blwyf. Yni law y mae

The designation, however, of some of the Church Festivals, derived no doubt from the Welsh colloquialism of the period, is quite independent of the English: (1) "The Nativity of our Lord or the Birthday of Christ, commonly called Christmas Day." Welsh: "Genedigaeth ein Harglwydd, neu Ddydd Nadolig Crist." "Christmas" is a Romish word, and connects the Festival with the "mass-of-Christ." The Welsh "Nadolig" is from the Latin natalicia, and connects the Festival with the great fact of the Nativity. The Welsh equivalent to "Christmas" would be, "offeren Crist." It is also colloquially termed "Gwyliau y Nadolig," or the "Festivals of the Nativity," from, no doubt, the three Saint Days that immediately follow Christmas Day. (2) "The Epiphany, or the Manifestation of Christ to the Gentiles." Welsh: "Dydd Gwyl Ystwyll, neu'r Seren-wyl, sef Ymddatgudd Crist i'r Cenhedloedd." The English "Epiphany" is derived from the Greek ἐπιφάνειν; the Welsh from the Latin stella = a star. In fact, the Festival is called the "Star-Festival" in the Welsh Prayer-Book. (3) Lent is derived from the old English Lenten, Anglo-Saxon lengten, lencten, spring, Lent, long, longer; or, possibly, from the German linde, mild; Dutch, lenten, to

---

holl dervynav y daiar ac ef a edrychodd vch vchder y mynyddoedd. Duw biav y moroedd ac efa id gwnaeth ai ddwylaw y seilawdd ef y dowarchen, a ddevwn ac yddolwn a syrthiwn gar bron duw, ac wylwn i yngwydd yr arglwydd an gwnaeth ni kanis yno yw yn harglwyd ni a ninav yw i bobyl," &c.

It is noteworthy that the Latin in the second paragraph is phonetically spelt according to the Welsh pronunciation. It stands for this: "Ave Maria, gratia plena, Dominus tecum, benedicta tu in mulieribus, et benedictus fructus ventris tui, Jesus Christus."

make mild, because the severity of the winter is then relaxed; and the Fast is so called because it always happens in the spring. Welsh: "Garawys." Some old writers have compared the Lenten season to man's earthly pilgrimage of trouble and care. If the derivation of "Garawys" be from "garw," rough, the Welsh name of the season conveys this idea, as in the hymn—

"My God, my Father, while I stray,
Far from my home, in life's *rough* way."

The term "Garawys" is, however, more correctly accepted as a corruption of "Quadragesima," having reference to the forty days of Lent. (4) "Good Friday." Welsh: "Dydd Gwener y Croglith," or, "The Friday of the Lesson of the Cross."[1] (5) Easter (an Anglo-Saxon word from Eastre, a goddess in honour of whom a festival was held in April). Welsh: "Pasg," retaining the old Jewish word Pasga, the Passover of the Old Testament.

These Welsh terms may have been handed down orally from the period of the early British Church. Nadolig, Garawys, Croglith, a'r Pasg, are terms now as colloquially common among Welsh people, as Christmas, Lent, Good Friday, and Easter are among the English.

"Priest" is rendered "offeiriad" in the Welsh Prayer-Book. The correct translation is "henadur," elder: "minister" is correctly translated "gweinidog." The translators of the Welsh Prayer-Book adopted the colloquial term "offeiriad,"

---

[1] In different countries, different names have been given to this day: Passion Friday, Still Friday, Great Friday, Black Friday, the Friday of the Cross, Adoration Day.

which implies, one who offers. The Welsh term
" offeren," for Mass, is of like derivation, as also
the English term offertory, still retained in the
Communion Service.[1] The clergy are more commonly termed "offeiriad" in Wales, than they are
"priests" in England.

The Psalms in the 1586 edition were translated
from the Hebrew, so we are told on the front page
of the Psalter. "Psallwyr nue Psalma David wedi
ei Gamberei-gan i'n nesaf ac' allit, a chadw'r bwyll,
i'r llythyr Ebrew: a'i ddosbarth wrth y drefn y
darlleir in yr Eccleis."[2]

---

[1] "Then shall the Priest return to the Lord's Table, and
begin the offertory "=" Yna y dychwel yr offeiriad at Fwrdd
yr Arglwydd, ac a ddechreua'r offrymiad."

[2] In the English Prayer-Book, Tyndal's translation is
preserved unto this day in the Communion Sentences, the
Commandments and the Psalms, as being clearer and
smoother, though not so accurately rendered.

CHAPTER XII.

BISHOP WILLIAM HUGHES of S. Asaph was
accused, in the year 1587, of misgoverning his
diocese, and of tolerating gross abuses. On inquiry,
it was found that the Bishop himself held sixteen
livings *in commendam ;* that most of the rich livings
in the diocese were in the possession of persons who
were non-resident ; and that only three preachers
resided upon their livings, viz. David Powell, Vicar
of Ruabon ; William Morgan, Vicar of Llanrhaiadr-
yn-mochnant ; and the Vicar of Llanfechain, an old
man about eighty years of age.

The original document now in the British
Museum, entitled, "A Discouerie of the present
estate of the Byshopprick of St. Asaph. Doctor
Hughes of Cātbr (Canterbury) first and afterwards
wēt to Cambridge," has no signature, but inferentially it was composed by some stranger, for the
writer refers to S. Asaph as " that Dioces."

The document—if it be a true bill—is a grave
indictment against Bishop Hughes. Without, however, minimizing the importance of the charges, it
should, in fairness, be stated that ten out of the
sixteen livings which he held *in commendam* were

sinecures. In consequence of the poverty of the see (valued then at £187 a year), Parker had authorized Bishop Hughes to hold *in commendam* the Archdeaconry of S. Asaph, the rectory of Llysfaen, which he had held before his elevation to the see, and other benefices to the value of £150 a year. The revenue of this Archdeaconry had been derived from livings with cure, and four sinecures; and the Bishop further took two benefices with cure, and four sinecure rectories with two chapelries attached, in satisfaction of the £150 a year. A similar complaint was made against Bishop Thomas Davies, in 1563. The decision of Archbishop Parker in that case tends, at least, to qualify the unmixed condemnation of Bishop Hughes. Neither was he so unmindful of the spiritual interests of his diocese as is often represented. In the case of Albany *v.* Bishop of S. Asaph,[1] we learn that he refused to institute a Mr. Bagshaw to the living of Whittington, vacant through the death of Rector Kyffin in 1585, on the ground that he did not understand Welsh sufficiently well to minister therein to the parishioners. Bishop Hughes investigated the ancient privileges of the diocese of S. Asaph, as appears from a document printed in Appendix No. I. of Browne Willis' *Survey of S. Asaph Cathedral;* and he was a benefactor to his Church, for he bequeathed lands and moneys, under certain conditions, in favour of S. Asaph Grammar School, by his will, dated 16th Oct. 1597; but the bequest was lost, because the conditions were not

[1] Reported in 1st Leonard, p. 39; and Crooke, Elizabeth, p. 119. (From the Whittington Registers.)

complied with.[1] Notwithstanding the abuse which has been heaped upon him for his alleged grasping, avaricious spirit—and he was not alone in this respect, for Bishop Richard Davies was not free from a similar charge [2]—his memory is entitled to the respect and gratitude of posterity, for the help he gave Morgan to bring to a successful issue the work of translating the Welsh Bible. After the death of Bishop Richard Davies, Bishop Hughes was the only one of the Welsh prelates who took any active part in that great and blessed work.

The non-residence complained of is, however, a dark spot in that page of the history of the diocese of S. Asaph, and reflects little credit on the administration of Bishop Hughes. That he should have appointed one Banks, in 1587, to the Deanery of S. Asaph, before he had attained the age of twenty-three years, and allowed the same man in 1582-84, when he was younger, to be sinecure rector of Caerwys and Llangwm; sinecure rector of Pennant, 1583-88; Canon, 1585-87; sinecure rector of Llansantffraid-yn-Mechain, 1585—1600; sinecure rector of Llandrillo-yn-Edeirnion, 1600-34, are glaring instances of the grossest abuse of

---

[1] Browne Willis' *Survey*, p. 107.

[2] "It is to be regretted that so distinguished a character should have given cause of complaint in the management of his diocese; but it is not to be concealed that he greatly impoverished the bishopric of S. David's to provide for his numerous family, as was complained of by his successor, who tells us, 'that all his lands even to his very doors were in lease by his predecessor; all the spiritual livings worth £10 a year advowsoned; all his houses, excepting one, down to the ground, and in great ruin'" (Williams' *Eminent Welshmen*, p. 109).

episcopal patronage. Inferentially, Dean Banks must have been in Orders before he was twenty-three years of age, for he published a sermon in 1586.[1] He was Dean of S. Asaph forty-seven years, from 1587 to 1634—a worthless man—and very different to his predecessor Hugh Evans, of whom Bishop Richard Davies said in his Return to Archbishop Parker, A.D. 1560, that he was one of the few "*concionatores evangelici*" in the diocese. If we compare the state of the diocese in 1560 with that in 1587, we shall find that out of one hundred and thirty-four clergy, there were only thirteen non-resident in 1560 ;[2] and out of as many, at least, in 1587, there were only three preachers in the whole diocese who resided on their livings! and Dr. Morgan was one of them. True, that the Return of 1560 only shows four out of the one hundred and thirty-four as favouring the Reformation ; but surely even such a ministry was far better than no ministry at all. The only lights in the whole diocese of S. Asaph at this time were Dr. Morgan and Dr. Powell, Vicar of Ruabon, who resided among their flocks. It seems almost incredible that the diocese should have been reduced to such a feeble state. The spirit of worldliness, so characteristic of the times of the Reformation, was not without its evil effects on the minds and actions of the clergy, as well as of the laity, in this and subsequent periods. In its practical effects—immediate and remote—the Reformation moved, like the pendulum of a clock, from one extreme to the other. From the zealous reaction against superstition it swung to the other

---

[1] *Hist. Dio. St. Asaph*, p. 242.
[2] See p. 61, Part I. of this Essay.

extreme of worldliness and indifference, of which the history of the diocese of S. Asaph in Morgan's time is a painful illustration.

Dr. Morgan was also a sinecurist, for, in addition to the Vicarage of Llanrhaiadr where he resided, he held the Rectory of Llanfyllin, to which he was promoted in 1579, on the resignation of Dr. David Powell, Vicar of Ruabon, who had also held it as a sinecure since 1571 ; the sinecure Rectory of Pennant Melangell, to which he was instituted July 10, 1588; and the sinecure of Denbigh, to which he was preferred in 1594. All these preferments were given to Dr. Morgan by Bishop Hughes.[1] Though these benefices were sinecures, it is probable that Dr. Morgan may have officiated there occasionally, especially at Llanfyllin and Pennant Melangell— two parishes on the confines of Llanrhaiadr ; while the inhabitants of Denbigh indulge in the belief that their ancestors had the privilege of hearing the voice of the learned translator of the Bible.

Dr. David Powell, one of Morgan's helpers in the work, was also a sinecurist ; for, in addition to the Vicarage of Ruabon, which he served, he held the Rectory of Llanfyllin, 1571-78; S.R. Llansant-ffraid, 1588. In view of the great dearth of scholars and Welsh preachers at this time, it is not improbable that Bishop Hughes may have made some arrangement with Dr. Powell and Dr. Morgan that they should minister occasionally in these parishes. If the memory of Bishop Hughes is censurable as a sinecurist, the memories of Drs.

---

[1] Letter of Bishop Humphryes to Ant. A. Wood, 1 col. 615, Lansdowne 983, f. 40, in the British Museum.

Powell and Morgan are not altogether free from similar blame.

The fact that the Church in Wales has survived all her manifold and sad misfortunes, is a proof of her divine mission. Of her it may be truly said, as Isaiah said of the Jewish Church of old—" Except the Lord of hosts had left us a very small remnant, we should have been as Sodom, and we should have been like unto Gomorrah " (Isaiah i. 9).

CHAPTER XIII.

A.D. 1588.

Publication of the first Welsh Bible—Morgan's Journey to London —Difficulties of Travelling—The Guest of Dean Goodman— Correcting the Press—Presents a Copy of his Translation to the Dean and Chapter of Westminster—Dedicates the Work to the Queen—Translation of the Latin Dedication with Notes—Salesbury and the Translation of the Bible—Some Criticisms on Morgan's Translation—The Dialect of the Welsh Bible.

" Dyma Fibl f'anwyl Iesu
    Dyma rodd deheulaw Duw;
Dengys hwn y ffordd i farw,
    Dengys hwn y ffordd i fyw ;
Dengys hwn y codwm erchyll
    Gafwyd draw yn Eden drist ;
Dengys hwn y ffordd i fywyd
    Trwy adnabod Iesu Grist."

DR. MORGAN went up to London in the year 1587, with his completed manuscript translation of the Old Testament, and the revision of Salesbury's translation of the New, to correct the press. It was printed in London, "by the Deputies of Christopher Barker, Printers to the Queen's most excellent Majestie, 1588"; with whom, no doubt, Archbishop Whitgift had caused arrangements to be made, before Morgan undertook his journey. The cost of printing was paid by the Archbishop out of his own private purse, as we are told in the

Dedication. "The Archbishop of Canterbury . . . prevailed upon me to proceed: and helped me with his purse, his influence and his counsel."

A journey to London, such as that from Llanrhaiadr, was surrounded with no small inconveniences in those days; and beset frequently with no little risk to life and limb. Such tedious journeys were generally undertaken during the summer months, and advantage was taken of the companies of drovers, who kept up a traffic with the metropolis. An unprotected party was less secure than a large company from attack by highwaymen, with whom the roads were everywhere infested; and who flourished unpunished,[1] to the

---

[1] The most famous group of banditti in Wales were the "Gwylliaid Cochion Mawddwy." The ordinary authorities having utterly failed to suppress the ruffians, Government issued a Commission, in 1554, to John Wyn of Gwydir and Lewis Owen to deal with them. Eighty out of the gang were captured, put on their trial, and convicted. The mother of two of the convicts made an earnest, but fruitless, appeal to Baron Owen to pardon one of her sons. Turning to the judge, she bared her bosom, and exclaimed, " These yellow breasts have given suck to those who shall wash their hands in your blood." The day of revenge came. Those of the gang who were still at large waylaid the Baron on his way to the Montgomeryshire Assizes, through these parts. They cut down trees and placed them across the road to obstruct its passage. As soon as the Baron and his escort came within reach, arrows were showered upon them from the ambuscade, to their utter discomfiture. The outlaws advanced, killed Baron Owen, leaving his body on the road with more than thirty wounds. One of the gang, remembering his mother's threat, turned back and literally washed his hands in the baron's blood. This cold-blood murder roused the authorities to vigorous action, which resulted in the complete extirpation of the whole band.

great terror of all who had to undertake long journeys to transact business.

Dr. Morgan was the guest of Dean Goodman at the Deanery, Westminster, during the whole year the work was passing through the press. Of the Dean's kindness and help he thus speaks in the Dedication—

"Gabriel Goodman, Dean of Westminster, 'an eminently good man' in fact as in name—and of most devoted piety, who as I read over again my translation, gave me such diligent attention that he very greatly helped me by his labour and advice ; presented me with several books and granted the use of all his others ; and for a whole year, while this book was in the press, entertained me hospitably, with the consent of his colleagues, a kindness indeed which the most Reverend Archbishop, of whom I have already made mention in my Letter most generously offered, but which the river Thames, which cuts off and separates his house from the press, compelled me to decline."

The personal supervision and correction of the press by Morgan himself were indispensable in a work which to the compositors was, in all probability, written in a foreign tongue. The postal arrangements also, at this time, were not such that the press could be corrected by post ; though they were greatly improved during the reign of Elizabeth ; when roads were opened, and couriers established throughout the kingdom. Three main roads were opened from London to Ireland, one terminating at Liverpool, and the other two at Holyhead. In 1558, the Government had decided that the master of the couriers should have the care of the letter-carriers, British and Foreign ; and the name of that officer was, in 1581, changed to Chief Post-master. The cost, however, of transmitting letters, and the Government dues, were very high during the first half of the reign of Elizabeth. Up to the year 1589, 1s. 8d. was the fee charged for every twenty miles, besides a charge of one penny per mile by the proprietors of the conveyance, according to the statute of Edward VI. The Government propounded a new scheme, by which the proprietors were paid 3s. a day, irrespective of distance. This sum was subsequently reduced to 2s. and later on to 1s. 6d. per day. Up to the year 1589—a year after the Welsh Bible was printed—these postal arrangements were confined to the public service.[1] So that Dr. Morgan's presence at the printing-office in London was an absolute necessity. The number of private letters was comparatively small, for the clergy and gentry were almost the only people who could write at that time ; and they delivered their letters by their own private messengers. Dr. Morgan had his own messenger in his correspondence with John Wyn ; and the latter sent his reply also by his own private messengers.

In the year 1588—a memorable one in the history of Wales and of the Welsh language—appeared the first translation of the entire Bible into the Welsh language. Eight hundred copies

---

[1] Great care was taken to seal letters in those days, and they were carefully tied with silk or cotton thread, so as to shield the ends from the inquisitive eye of the courier, who was also the news herald ; and his appearance in town and village was the signal for the gathering round him of crowds, anxious to hear news from a distance. The courier then, as the postman is now, was at all times and in all places a welcome visitor.

were printed in black letter, small folio size. The number was scarcely sufficient to supply the parish churches of Wales each with a copy.

Morgan must have hailed with inexpressible joy the completion of the great work of his life—a work which, as regards its influence on the moral and religious character of the people for whom it was intended, is probably unrivalled in the history of Christendom. The translator was only forty-one years of age when his Welsh translation of the Word of God was put up in all the parish churches of Wales. A young man. But a great worker. Truly "the honourable age is not that which is of long time, neither that which is measured by the number of years." [1] Morgan did not live to see the fruit of the labour of his soul in the spiritual welfare of his countrymen. He lighted a candle in Wales which has never been put out ; but has continued to burn with greater brightness in each succeeding generation. Even the ardent zeal and patriotism of Dr. Morgan would perhaps have scarcely carried him so far as to hope, much less to predict, that in three hundred years from that memorable year of grace, 1588, thousands of his countrymen, scattered all over the world, would join to celebrate the Tercentenary of the publication of his translation of the Bible into their language—a movement based not only on grand memories of the past, but prompted also by the throbbings of the *existing* influence and life-giving power of the Welsh Bible, wherever the Welsh language is spoken. The fact that the work which Morgan accomplished in 1588 is, in 1891, a living power,

---

[1] Wisdom of Solomon iv. 8.

is without doubt the best monument to the character, the labour, and the worth of the man.

Before leaving London for his home, Morgan presented the Dean and Chapter of Westminster with the copy of his Welsh Bible which is still in their library, and is specially interesting above all other existing copies. The corrigenda at the end is believed to be in the handwriting of Dr. Jaspar Gryffydd of Ruthin. The translator's Latin Dedication of the work to the Queen contains in his own words, a history of the trials, opposition, helps and encouragement he experienced and received, while engaged on the work. The following translation of it will be read, therefore, with interest—

" To The
Most Illustrious, Potent and Serene Princess
Elizabeth.
By the Grace of God, Queen of England, France, and Ireland, Defender of the True and Apostolic [1]
Faith, &c.
Greeting and eternal Benediction in the Lord:

" How much your Majesty owes to Almighty God, most noble Princess (not to speak of your wealth, your power and your admirable endowments of birth and intellect) is abundantly testified not only by that most rare grace, wherein you so excel, that varied learning, with

---

[1] Morgan does not quote this title as it was given by the Pope to Henry VIII., which is simply "Defender of the Faith." That title was given to the King for defending the doctrine of the Church of Rome against Luther. It was, doubtless, not accidental that Morgan qualified the Papal title with the words "True and Apostolic." The Queen was a " Defender of the true and Apostolic Faith," in the encouragement she gave to the unrestricted use of the Word of God, of which this Welsh edition is a proof.

which you are pre-eminently adorned, that happy peace which you enjoy above your neighbours, and that divine protection, which can never be sufficiently acknowledged, whereby you have both lately put your savage foes to flight,[1] and have ever most fortunately escaped many great dangers; but also, most of all, by that distinguished piety, famous all the world over, with which He has imbued and adorned your majesty, and that most forward zeal for both the propagation and the defence of true religion, wherewith you have ever been influenced. For (to pass over for the present other nations and the rest of your noble deeds) what an affectionate care your Majesty has for your British subjects, this alone is sufficient to testify through all time, that you have not only graciously permitted, but have anxiously ratified it with the authority of the High Parliament of this most famous realm,—that both the Testaments of the Holy Word of God,—that is to say, both the Old and the New, —together with the Book that prescribes the Form of Public Prayer and the Order for the Administration of the Sacraments,—should be translated into the British tongue.   And this at the same time exposes our own sloth and indolence, that we could neither be moved by so grave a necessity, nor compelled by so beneficial a law, from leaving so long, almost untouched, a matter of the very greatest possible importance.   For it was the Liturgy with the New Testament only, that the Reverend Father, Richard, of pious memory, Bishop of S. David's, with the aid[2] of William Salesbury, who above all men has

---

[1] The defeat of the Spanish Armada, which was on the 28th July, 1588.   The Welsh Bible was evidently published after that event, in the same year; and this Dedication was drawn up at the Westminster Deanery House.

[2] Morgan speaks of Salesbury as an assistant to Bishop Davies, and not as one taking a leading part in the work of translation.   His testimony, inasmuch as it is contemporary, is final on this point.   Moses Williams, as quoted in *Llyfry-*

deserved well of our Church, translated into the British language some twenty years ago. How greatly he benefited our countrymen thereby cannot easily be told. For, besides that the common people, by comparing together the British and English Scriptures, became more conversant with the English tongue; he contributed very largely, by that labour, alike to the teaching and the learning of the truth. For at that time hardly any one was able to preach in the British tongue; because the terms in which the sacred mysteries treated of in Holy Scripture should be explained in that language, had either entirely disappeared—swept away, as it were, in Lethean waters—or had lain hidden and buried under the dust of disuse; so that neither the teachers could clearly explain what they would, nor the hearers satisfactorily understand the things that were explained.[1] Besides which, having been little used to the Scriptures, they were not able to distinguish between the testimony of the Scriptures and their exposition; so that when they crowded eagerly to hear the sermons and attended to them diligently, they had to go away for the most part in uncertainty

---

ddiaeth-y-Cymry, p. 21, states that Bishop Davies was the assistant of Salesbury. Tegid (*Bedd Gwr Duw*, p. 24) attributes the leading part in the work to the Bishop. The probabilities of the case point in this direction also; his position as Bishop, his superior knowledge of Welsh over Salesbury, and the fact that the latter resided with the Bishop at the palace, corroborate the testimony of Morgan, that Bishop Davies did the work "with the aid of William Salesbury."

[1] Evidently Welsh preaching had long fallen into disuse, and the theological character of the Welsh language almost obliterated. The most convincing arguments of the influence of the Welsh Bible on the Welsh language are, that it has reversed the state of things which Morgan describes, and that the language now abounds in Biblical phrases, which have become so ingrained into the Welsh mind, as to be applied sometimes, with doubtful propriety, to secular subjects.

and doubt, like men who had found a rich treasure which
they could not dig out—or who had been to a sumptuous
banquet, which they were not allowed to partake of.
But now, through the exceeding goodness of Almighty
God, and your Majesty's gracious care, and through the
watchful forethought of our Bishops [1] and the labour and
industry of this your translator, provision has been made
for having both the preachers more numerous and better
prepared, and the hearers more easily taught. And as
both these objects are dear to the heart of the pious,—
so neither of them has hitherto corresponded to their
wishes. For inasmuch as that earlier Testament, which,
is an undeveloped prediction, a veiled type, an unerring
witness of the Later—has up to the present time been
wanting to our countrymen ; how many examples alas !
lie half hidden ! how many promises are concealed ! how
many consolations are obscured ! how many the counsels,
exhortations, warnings and testimonies to the truth,—are
unwillingly missed by our people, whom your Majesty
reigns over, cares for, and loves; and whose eternal
salvation, hateful to Satan only and his satellites, has
hitherto been grievously endangered, seeing that every
one lives by faith, and faith cometh by hearing; and
hearing by the Word of God; which hitherto lying hid in a
foreign tongue has awakened but a slight echo in the heart
of our fellow countrymen. When therefore, I saw that
the translation of the rest of the Scriptures was so useful,
nay so necessary (though long deterred by the sense alike
of my own weakness and of the greatness of the subject,
as well as of the evil affection of certain persons),[2] I

---

[1] This has, probably, reference only to the two Bishops of
North Wales, whom Morgan names further on. Bishop
Richard Davies died in 1582, and was succeeded by Marma-
duke Middleton, an Englishman, and the Bishop of Llandaff,
Wm. Blethin, was also an Englishman.

[2] This has reference, no doubt, to the opposition which

yielded to the appeals of good men, and allowed myself
to be persuaded [1] to undertake this most important,
troublesome, and, to many, unacceptable work. But
hardly had I taken it in hand, when, overwhelmed by the
difficulty of the task and the greatness of the expense, I
should have given in at the very threshold, so to say, and
brought only the Pentateuch through the press, had it
not been that the most Reverend Father in Christ, the
Archbishop of Canterbury—that most excellent Patron
of literature, most keen champion of the Truth, and most
prudent Guardian of Order and seemliness (who from
the time when he presided, under your Majesty, with so
much prudence and justice, over your British subjects,[2]
and observed their obedience and intelligence, has ever
regarded them with favour, as indeed they do ever sing
his praise) prevailed upon me to proceed : and helped
me with his purse, his influence, and his counsel. And
following his example, other good men have given me
very great assistance. And when moved, supported and
ever aided by their encouragement, industry and labours,
I had not only translated the whole of the Old Testament,
but had also revised the New, which abounded largely

Morgan received from his parishioners to the work of translation,—an opposition which was to him disheartening, and
delayed the work.

[1] The undertaking of the work of translation was not, as is
sometimes supposed, spontaneous on the part of Dr. Morgan :
he was urged on by "the appeals of good men"—chiefly by
his own Bishop, to undertake the work. This is, on the one
hand, a testimony to his high scholarship and qualifications
for the work ; and, on the other, a testimony to his own
modest humility and sense of unworthiness to undertake it.

[2] This has reference to the time when Whitgift was Vice-
President of the Council for the Marches of Wales, the
duties of which brought him frequently to Wales, and he was
popular in the principality. The encouragement he gave to
Morgan was based upon a knowledge of the people, and a
deep regard for them.

in an un-emended orthography, I hesitated in doubt as
to whom it was right and fitting I should dedicate them.
And when I think of my own unworthiness and look
upon the exceeding splendour of your Majesty, in whom
I recognise a bright reflection as it were of Him, whose
vicegerent you are : I dread to approach a splendour so
sacred.   But on the other hand the dignity of the subject
itself, which of its own right as it were claims your
patronage, inspires me with a new courage.   And in the
next place,—seeing you have already deigned with such a
righteous, gracious, and royal will to take under your
charge the one Testament in its British garb,—I hold it
would be unwise, wrong and ungrateful to seek a different
Patron for the other.   Besides which, I think that where
the subjects so entirely cohere and agree, they should not
be separated, but that being in truth the same, they
should have their copies laid up in the same library.
And that your Majesty may concur in this view I humbly
ask and entreat ; nay, I plead with the most earnest
prayers that you will graciously favour my efforts, which
are such as rest on the authority of your laws, conduce to
the salvation of your people and aim at the glory of our
GOD : and such as I trust will prove not only an abiding monument of your zeal for the truth and regard for
your British subjects, but also a token of their most
devoted affection for your Majesty.   And, if for the sake
of preserving agreement, any maintain that our countrymen should learn the English tongue, rather than that
the Scriptures should be translated into our own : I
would have them in their zeal for unity, to be more careful
lest they hinder the truth, and more anxious, while promoting concord, not to put religion on one side.   For,
although it is much to be desired that the inhabitants of
the same island should be of the same speech and
language ; it must equally be borne in mind, that to
effect this end, so much time and trouble is required, that

to be willing, much less to suffer God's people, to perish
in the meantime from hunger of His Word—were both
barbarous and cruel. Moreover, there can be no doubt
that unity is more effectually promoted by similarity and
agreement in religion, than in speech. Besides, to prefer
unity to piety, expediency to religion, and a kind of
external concord among men, to that heavenly peace
which the Word of GOD impresses on men's souls,
shows but little piety. Last of all, how unwise are they,
who fancy that the prohibition of the Word of GOD in
the mother-tongue can avail anything towards the learning
of another. For, unless religion be taught in the vulgar
tongue, it will be hidden and unknown. For, where one
is ignorant of the thing itself, he cannot know its use or
sweetness, or its worth, and he will undergo no trouble
to acquire it. Wherefore your Majesty is implored not
to be prevented (which I am sure you will not be) from
enlarging your benefits to those whom you have begun to
bless; but that you will gratify with the New Testament
those whom you have enriched with the Old, and will
grant to those to whom you have given the one breast of
truth, the other also; and will endeavour to perfect what
you have been zealous to effect : viz. that all your
subjects may hear in their own language the wonderful
works of GOD, and that every tongue may praise Him.
May our Heavenly Father, who knows how to adorn, in
the person of your Majesty, human weakness, the female
sex and the virgin character with such heroic virtues,
that you have hitherto stood forth as a comfort to the
miserable, a terror to your enemies, and a very Phœnix to
the world,—graciously grant that you may be so governed
by His Spirit, so adorned with divine gifts, and ever
hereafter protected under the wings of the Most High
that you may continue a long-lived Mother in Israel, a
pious nurse of the Church; and being ever safe from
your enemies may yourself prove the enemy of every vice,

to the eternal glory of Almighty GOD, to whom be dominion and honour and praise for ever and ever. Amen.

> " Your most serene Majesty's,
> " With all reverence, most obedient,
> " WILLIAM MORGAN.

" The Names of those who have more especially endeavoured to promote this work—

" The Reverend Fathers, the Bishops of S. Asaph and Bangor, who have both of them lent me the books I asked for, and have condescended to examine, weigh and approve of the work.

" Gabriel Goodman, Dean of Westminster.

" So also these gave help not to be slightly spoken of—

" David Powel, Doctor of Divinity.

" Edmund Price, Archdeacon of Merioneth.

" Richard Vaughan, Provost of S. John's Hospital at Lutterworth."

Such were the forcible and dignified terms in which Morgan dedicated his translation to the Queen. Two names are conspicuous by their absence from the list of those who, the translator tells us, "endeavoured to promote this work"— Bishop Richard Davies and William Salesbury. Morgan refers to them as " deserving well of their Church," in the work they did together. But Davies died in 1581, before Morgan had done much of the translation. Of the history of Salesbury after his dispute with, and separation from, Davies, little or nothing is known. Sir John Wyn says that he outlived that event twenty-four years, " but gave over writing (more was the pity), for he was a rare scholar, and especially an hebrician, whereof there was not many in those days."[1] This would place Salesbury's death about the year 1593 —five years after the publication of Morgan's translation. He appears to have withdrawn entirely from all literary work in the Welsh language, and from public life. There is some reason for believing that Salesbury felt disappointed that his literary labours in the Welsh language were not appreciated.

The overthrow of the Spanish Armada, to which Morgan refers in his Dedication, happened in the same year as the publication of his Bible; but, of. course, before he had written the Dedication. He was in London at the time, correcting his proof-sheets; and was doubtless present at the national thanksgiving service held in S. Paul's Cathedral for the victory. As the guest of the Dean of Westminster, a place would be provided for him in the Cathedral on that auspicious occasion.

The Hebrew Bible from which Morgan is said to have made his translation is now in the possession of Lady Llanover. It contains no marginal notes, as stated in *Enwogion y Ffydd*, vol. i. p. 61.

Hebrew was a rare study in Morgan's time. Even Greek was then only a new introduction into our universities, owing to the fall of Constantinople. Sir John Wyn[2] asserts that Morgan "was a good scholar, both a grecian and a hebrecian." He, however, made much use of the Hebrew text, through the Latin interlinear version of Pagninus; an instance of which may be seen in 2 Kings vii. 1: "Sat o beillieid." The Hebrews had no such measure, but seah; and *sat* is taken from Pagninus—the only one that has it; and he took it from the LXX. σατον.

[1] *Memoirs*, p. 94.   [2] *Ibid.* p. 96.

I

The Welsh language was in a state of transition in Morgan's time. The difference between the Welsh of the sixteenth and nineteenth centuries is probably greater than the corresponding differ- ence in English. Notwithstanding the many diffi- culties which stood in the way of its translation, the Welsh Bible has always been regarded as the most valuable book in the language; and there can be little doubt that the Welsh translation is a nearer approach than the English is to the original Hebrew. The Welsh has retained the natural simplicity and characteristics of the Hebrew; *e.g.* the repeating of a verb twice over when special emphasis is required is retained in the Welsh trans- lation, *e.g.* Gen. ii. 17, "Gan farw y bydi farw"; iii. 16, "Gan amlhâu yr amlhaf"; xliv. 28, "Gan larpio y llarpiwyd." The English translation has: "Thou shalt surely die"; "I will greatly multiply"; "Surely he is torn in pieces." The Hebrew and the Welsh have: "Dying, thou shalt die"; "Increasing, I will increase"; "Torn, he has been torn."

An instance a'so of the copiousness of the vocabulary of Morgan's translation appears in I Sam. xvii. 37: "Yr Arglwydd, yr hwn a'm hachu- bodd i o grafangc y llew, ac o balf yr arth, efe a'm hachub i o law y Philistiad hwn." Here an appropriate instrument is given to each. The claw, or crafangc, to the lion; the paw, or palf, to the bear; and the hand, or llaw, to the man. The parallel passage in English is not so copious: "The Lord that delivered me out of the paw of the lion, and the paw of the bear, he will deliver me out of the hand of this Philistine."

Morgan in many instances has anticipated the corrections of the last English revision. The late Bishop Thirlwall of S. David's, himself a member of that Revision Committee, said—and the statement appeared in the public prints during his lifetime—that he never decided finally on the correct rendering of a verse without consulting the Welsh Bible. The readings and renderings preferred and recommended by the American Committee in the last revision of the English New Testament, have in many cases been anticipated in the Welsh Bible also, *e.g.* Matt. ix. 6 ; *i.e.* "awdurdod" ($\dot{\epsilon}\xi o \nu \sigma i a \nu$) "i faddeu pechodau," authority instead of "power to forgive sins." Luke viii. 33, "a foddwyd" ($\dot{a}\pi\epsilon\pi\nu i\gamma\eta$), "drowned" instead of "choked."

A curious illustration of an oversight is the omission in Morgan's translation of verse 44 in the fifth chapter of the Gospel according to S. Matthew : " Cerwch eich gelynion " = " Love your enemies." Verse 6 of the eighth chapter of the Gospel according to S. John is omitted altogether : " Eithr yr Jesu wedi ymgrymmu tua'r llawr, a ysgrifenodd a'i fys ar y ddaear, heb gymmeryd arno eu clywed." Another instance of carelessness occurs in Matt. xvi. 10, where Morgan renders $\tau\hat{\omega}\nu \ \tau\epsilon\tau\rho a\kappa\iota\sigma\chi\iota\lambda i\omega\nu$ " saith mil," for pedair mil, *i.e.* four thousand.

Though Morgan and the Welsh translators that preceded him (Hewett excepted), as well as their helpers, were North Walians, the dialect of the Welsh Bible is largely, though not altogether, that of South Wales. They probably followed the *literary* language of their day, most of which was written by South Walians. But it is an exaggeration to say that the translators of the Welsh Bible wrote in the colloquial dialect of South Wales. That would have been impossible, because they were unacquainted with it, not having resided there. Bishop Richard Davies and Salesbury, it is true, resided for two years together at Abergwili, engaged on the work of translation; but they were North Walians, and Bishop Morgan did not go to Llandaff for seven years after he had published his translation of the Bible. It would, however, have been undesirable, had it been possible, to introduce colloquialisms of any kind, whether from North or South Wales; for this would not have added to the purity of the language of the translation. Notwithstanding that the Welsh Bible embraces two dialects—the South Wales dialect preponderating—the language is quite intelligible to the inhabitants of the two divisions of the Principality, and is a centre of union between them.

The following instances may be interesting—

The word " bâd," the term used for a " boat " in the Welsh Bible, is South Wales Welsh. " Cwch " is the word in North Wales. The termination " es " for " od," as " dodes," " rhoddes," is South Wales, *e. g.* Gen. xxxiii. 5, " Y plant a roddes Duw." We have instances of both dialects in S. John iii. 16, " Canys felly y carodd Duw y byd, fel y *rhoddodd* efe." S. John v. 27, " Ac a *roddes* awdurdod iddo." There are also, on the other hand, expressions used in North Wales, and never used in South Wales, *e. g.* " Ymroi," in the sense of " giving way," yielding (1 Tim. iii. 8, " Nid yn ymroi i win lawer "), for which the South Wales dialect has " ymollwng."

The word " brwnt " in South Wales dialect signifies anything " filthy "; in North Wales it

THE DIALECT OF THE WELSH BIBLE.

frwnt lydded frwnt etto " = " He which is filthy, let
him be filthy still."   " Dyn brwnt ": N. Wales =
unkind, cruel man ; S. Wales = dirty, filthy man.
" Budr " is the term in North Wales for filth, and
the Welsh Bible uses it in this sense in Is. iv. 4,
" Golchi budreddi" = "wash away the filth"; Zech.
iii. 3, " Dillad budron " = " filthy garments "; 1
Peter v. 2, " Budr-elw " = " filthy lucre."

So also the word "gwirion" has a different meaning in the two dialects.   " Dyn Gwirion " in North
Wales signifies " a foolish man "; in South Wales
"an innocent man."   There is one instance, in Ps.
xix. 7, of the word being used in the sense of the
North Wales dialect, " Yn gwneuthur y gwirion yn
doeth " = " making wise the simple." But there are
many instances of its being used in the South
Wales dialect : " Gwn na'm berni yn wirion " (Job
ix. 28)= " I know thou wilt not hold me innocent";
Ps. xv. 5, " Gwobr yn erbyn y gwirion " = " taketh
reward against the innocent "; Matt. xxvii. 4, " Gan
fradychu gwaed gwirion"="in that I have betrayed
innocent blood "; Jer. xix. 4, " A llenwi o honynt
y lle hwn o waed gwirioniaid "[1] = " and have filled
the place with the blood of innocents."

The word is also used in this sense in the
Baptismal Service of the Church of England,
" Pa wedd y cynghora Efe i bob dyn ganlyn eu
gwiriondeb hwy."   Also in the Interlude for Good

[1] " Dydd Gwyl y Gwironiaid," *i.e.* Innocent's Day, in the
Prayer-Book, is, however, sometimes in North Wales understood by some people in the North Wales acceptation of
the term, " Gwirion," and explained as the "Feast-Day of
Fools " !

Friday (Enterlute y Croglith) of pre-Reformation times—

S. EIRW (The Centurion).

" Gwirion fab Duw y-dyw hwn
Yn dioddef i bassiwn
A dioddefodd farfol loes
Ar y groes, mi a'i gwyddwn."

So also in the Prayer-Book, in the third commandment, " Nid gwirion gan yr Arglwydd yr hwn a gymmero ei enw ef yn ofer." In the Welsh Bible the word is, however, rendered "dieuog" (Exodus xx. 7), *i. e.* "guiltless," as in the English Bible.

Sir Thomas Salesbury, in his preface to Middleton's Metrical Psalms, published in 1603, says that among other books ready for the press he had a "Testament wedi ei ddiwy-gio gan Esgob Llanelwy." "Testament improved by the Bishop of S. Asaph." This was doubtless Morgan's manuscript revision of Salesbury's translation. It was, however, never published, owing probably to the Bishop's death in the following year.

CHAPTER XIV.

Some Account of the Men who helped Morgan—His Portrait—
Whitgift—Martin Marprelate Tracts—Penry—Bishop Hughes
of S. Asaph—Bishop Bellott of Bangor—Dean Goodman—Dr.
Powell — Archdeacon Prys — Dr. Richard Vaughan and Dr.
Henry Rowlands.

THE translator of the Welsh Bible has handed
down to posterity the names of those who helped
him to bring his great work to a successful
issue, and deserve to be held in veneration by all
Welshmen. A careful but fruitless search has
been made of all the old prints in the British
Museum, the Bodleian, Lambeth, and Peniarth
Libraries, and of the collections of many private
individuals, for a portrait of Morgan. It is very
doubtful if his portrait was ever taken. The inventory of his goods and chattels, taken after his
death, has no reference to one. If there was a
painting at the Palace, S. Asaph, at the time of
his death, his wife or nephew most likely possessed
themselves of it. If the Bishop's wife survived
him, as she probably did, there is no clue to her
whereabouts after her husband's death to trace a
portrait in the possession of any surviving relatives.
Evan Morgan, the Bishop's nephew, survived his
uncle many years, and was Vicar of Mold in 1612;
rector of Denbigh, 1615 ; and Prebendary of Meifod
in 1617.

Of the eight men forming the "cloud of witnesses" around the publication of the first Welsh Bible, the face most conspicuous by its absence is that of the great central figure—Bishop Morgan, and the one posterity would have rejoiced to recognize as the face of the great benefactor of his country. In the absence of a portrait, and even of a tradition respecting his countenance and stature, no idea can be formed of his features and form.

First on the list stands the name of John Whitgift, Archbishop of Canterbury. Born in 1530, and educated under his uncle, Robert Whitgift, Abbot of the monastery of Wellow, near Grimsby, young Whitgift removed to S. Anthony's School, London, and was lodged with his aunt in S. Paul's Churchyard, who was married to one of the vergers at the cathedral. She, as well as the Canons of S. Paul's, entreated Whitgift to attend mass; but, influenced by the spirit of the Reformation, he refused. His continued resistance to their combined importunities became so intolerable to the aunt, that at last she turned him out of doors, attributing all her losses and domestic misfortunes to her harbouring such a heretic under her roof; and when they parted she told Whitgift that "she thought at first she had received a saint into her house, but now she perceived he was a devil." From London he turned his face homewards to Lincolnshire; his uncle, the Abbot, perceiving the progress he had made, advised he should be sent to the University of Cambridge, where he matriculated in the year 1548 or 1549, at Queen's College. He was removed to Pembroke Hall, and was there under the tuition of the celebrated martyr John Bradford. He was elected Fellow of Peterhouse in 1553-4, and took his Master's degree in 1557. In the year 1560 he took Holy Orders, and soon after preached his first sermon at S. Mary's before the University, from Rom. i. 16: "I am not ashamed of the Gospel of Christ"; which gave great and general satisfaction. Whitgift became Margaret Professor in 1563 (a year before Morgan's matriculation), and was in high repute at Cambridge as a preacher and administrator. In 1567 he was appointed Regius Professor of Divinity; Dean of Lincoln, 1571; Bishop of Worcester, 1577. His *Admonition to the Parliament, newlie augmented by the Authour, as by conference shall appear*,[1] stands in the same relation to the organic principles of the Church of England as Jewell's *Apology* does to her doctrine.

On the death of Grindal, Whitgift was promoted to the Archbishopric in 1583. His first and chief care was to establish more uniformity in the Church. With this object he moved for an ecclesiastical commission, and issued articles of inquiry to all the bishops of the province, in which they were enjoined to summon all such clergy in their dioceses as were suspected of inconformity, and to require them to answer those articles severally, upon oath *ex officio mero*, to subscribe to the Queen's supremacy, the Book of Common Prayer, and the XXXIX. Articles of Religion.

---

[1] "Imprinted at London by Henrie Bynneman, for Humphrey Toy, Anno 1573." This was the same printer who had undertaken and printed, five years before this, Salesbury's Welsh Testament.

In the same year that the Welsh Bible was, printed appeared the Martin Marprelate Tracts, noted for their violent and bitter attacks on the Church of England, in which also Whitgift was severely handled. They were written by a club of writers who had possessed themselves of a private press, which they carried about with them to prevent detection.   No one was allowed to print then without a license, and all publications had to undergo the scrutiny of the Archbishop, or the Bishop of London.

John Penry, a native of Breconshire, was suspected of being the author of the tract signed "Martin Marprelate," which gave the name to the movement.   The title, which shows the style of the writer, runs : "Certain demonstrative conclusions set down and collected by Martin Marprelate the Great, serving as a manifest and sufficient confutation of all that ever the College of Catercaps, with their whole band of Clergy-Priest, have, or can bring for the defence of their ambitious and Anti-Christian Prelacy. Published by Martin Junior, 1589, in octavo, and dedicated to John Kankerbury "[1] (i.e. Whitgift). It was, however, never proved that Penry had any connection with these tractarians ; and his defenders urge that the style is entirely different to his, and that he never wrote anonymously. The writer of the article in *Enwogion y Ffyd*,[2] controverts this last statement, and says he had in his possession a tract entitled, " M. Sorne[3] laid open in his Coulers," 1588, which the same

---

[1] Wood's *Athen. Oxon.* under " Penry."
[2] Vol. i. p. 79, " Penry."
[3] Dr. Sorne was one of Whitgift's disciples.

writer attributes to Penry; and adduces this as an instance of his publishing anonymously.

In a letter to Lord Burleigh, written only seven days before his execution, Penry says: "I am a poor young man, born and bred in the mountains of Wales. I am first, since the last springing up of the Gospel in this latter age, that laboured to have the blessed seed thereof sown in these barren mountains."

Penry was about thirty-four years of age when he wrote this; Dr. Morgan about forty-six; Archdeacon Prys fifty-two; Dr. David Powell forty-one; the three considerably older than Penry, and devoted ministers of Christ in the principality; ministering to the population in the vernacular—which there is no proof that Penry ever did—and his ministrations in Wales must have been in English. So that in point of time and language, Penry could not justly claim to have been "the first who laboured to have the blessed seed of the Gospel" sown in Wales. Surely the translation of the Word of God into "the language understanded of the people," was the greatest of all efforts to sow the seed of the *Gospel*. It is probable, however, that Penry may have meant nothing more than his efforts to preach and disseminate the theological views which *he* had imbibed; and that he was the pioneer of Nonconformity in Wales. If so, his meaning is clear and correct.

The Privy Council issued a warrant in 1590 for Penry's apprehension, on the charge of being an enemy to the State; whereupon he fled to Scotland, returning to England three years later, when he was apprehended, in hiding, at Stepney. The papers found in his possession at the time of his apprehension formed an additional basis of the charges brought against him; but were not, according to the ruling of Lord Keeper Pickering, libellous. He was condemned and executed on the 25th May, 1593.

Whitgift was one of the three judges who signed the death-warrant, and he has not escaped the censure of posterity for the part he played. That there was a gross miscarriage of justice cannot be denied; and in that view only can we regard his action in the matter. He was not dealing with the case in a personal or theological sense; but merely in his official capacity, with two other judges.

The Archbishop died on the 29th February, 1604. On his death-bed he said: "And now, O Lord, my soul is rejoiced that I die in a time wherein I had rather give up to God an account of my bishopric, than any longer to exercise it among men."[1] He was buried in the parish church of Croydon on the 27th March, where a monument, with inscription, was erected to his memory, which has been recently restored.

The second person whom Morgan mentions among his helpers is Bishop Hughes of S. Asaph, of whom we have already spoken. He was the son of Hugh ap Cynnic, by Gwenllian, daughter of John Vychan ap John ap Gruffydd ap Owen Pygott, and was born in Carnarvonshire. He died October, 1600, and was buried in the choir of S. Asaph Cathedral, without any inscription to his

---

[1] *Biographia Evangelica*, p. 351.

memory.[1]   There is in the British Museum a good impression of his official seal: 3 × 2½ inches; pointed oval; divided into two parts by a horizontal line. In the upper part the sacrifice of Isaac; below, the inscription—

AGNUS . DEI . TOLLIT . PECCATA . MUNDI.

In the lower part, an ornamental shield of arms. Per . pale . *dex.* two Keys endorsed in saltire. SEE . OF . ST . . ASAPH . *Sinister,* a savage's head affrontee erased, wreathed about the temples, on a chief three roses HUGHES.

SIGILLUM . GVLIELI . HUGHES . EPISCOPI . ASAPHENSIS.

Hugh Bellott, Bishop of Bangor, 1585—1595, is also named as one of his helpers.   Bellott was one of the translators of the English Bible.   One of those clergy who never shook off the monastic austerities, he would on no account admit a female into his family.[2]   He was translated to Chester in 1595, where he died in less than a year after his translation; and was buried in the chancel of Wrexham church, where there is a recumbent effigy over his grave.   The effigy is much abraded, and a peculiar one, bearing apparently on the Vestiarian controversy, begun in 1564, and not

[1] Bishop Hughes' daughter and heiress, Ann, married the youngest son of Sir Thomas Mostyn, from whom are descended the Mostyns of Rhyd (Wood's *Athen. Oxon.*).

[2] *Royal Tribes of Wales*, p. 22.

yet settled. The Bishop is represented in the post-Reformation vestments, the rochet, and chimere ; over which he wears the academical habit, a close scarlet gown of a Doctor of Divinity of Cambridge ; round his neck is a short ruff, and fur or ermine tippet falling down between the shoulders. The inscription on the tomb is—

Spe certa gloriosæ resurrectionis hic in Domino ob-dormit Reverendus in Christo Pater D. Hugo Bellott, Sacrae Theologiae Doctor ex antiqua familia Bellotorum de Morton in Comitatu Cestriae oriundus : quem ob singularem in Deum pietatem, vitae integritatem, prudentiam, et doctrinam, Regina Elizabetha primum ad Episcopatum Bangorensem, in quo X annos sedit, postea ad Episcopatum Cestriensem transtulit, ex quo post paucos menses Christus in coelestem patriam evocavit Anno Domini 1596, ætatis suæ 54. Cuthbertus Bellott fratri optimo charissimo mæstissimus posuit.

There was an effigy of Archbishop Grindal, similarly habited, in Croydon Church, destroyed by fire some years ago, and another of Bishop Carew in Exeter Cathedral.

Gabriel Goodman, Dean of Westminster, was one of Morgan's best friends, and of whom he speaks with affection and regard. The Dean was born in 1528 at Ruthin, and educated at S. John's College, Cambridge. A personal friend of Lord Burleigh, he became Dean of Westminster, A. D. 1561. He was one of the principal ecclesiastics of the reign of Elizabeth, for the furtherance and consolidation of the Reformation; and distinguished himself by his zeal as a member of the High Commission Court, which made him unpopular, and

stood in the way of his promotion to the Bishopric
of London in 1570. Parker recommended him to
the Queen in 1575, for the Bishopric of Norwich, in
preference even to Whitgift, and others, as superior
in "learning, life and governance," but without
success ; he had the misfortune to incur the displeasure of Leicester, which proved an obstacle to
his promotion. Dean Goodman translated the
first Epistle to the Corinthians in the Bishop's
Bible, published in 1568. About the year 1584
his name was again put forward as deserving of a
mitre in connection with the sees of Worcester,
Chichester, and Rochester. Christ's Hospital at
Ruthin, in 1590, and the Grammar School, in 1595,
were founded by the Dean, and endowed with the
tithes of Ruthin and Llanrhydd, which he redeemed
at a high price from the lay impropriator. He
died June 17, 1601, aged seventy-three years, and
was buried in Westminster Abbey.

Dean Goodman has, on the sinister side of his
Coat of Arms, the double-headed eagle, displayed,
like Bishop Morgan.

Dr. David Powell, Vicar of Ruabon, another of
the helpers mentioned by Morgan, was born in
Denbighshire about the year 1552, and educated
at Oxford.[1] He was made Prebendary of S.
Asaph ; Rector of Llanfyllin ; Vicar of Meifod.
Powell took the degree of B.D. in 1582, and D.D.
in 1583. He died in 1598, and was buried in
Ruabon parish church.

[1] Jane, the granddaughter of Dr. Powell, married the
grandson of Sir John Wyn of Gwydir, with whom the
Baronetage became extinct. His wife was heiress of Watstay,
the name of which she changed into Wynnstay.

Edmund Prys, Archdeacon of Merioneth, was an intimate friend of Morgan, and received from him "help that was not to be lightly spoken of," in the work of translation.

The Archdeacon was born in 1541, at Gerddi Bluog, Llandecwyn, Merionethshire, and was educated at S. John's College, Cambridge, where he graduated. He was Rector of Ffestiniog, in 1572; Rector of Llanenddwyn, Merionethshire, 1580; Archdeacon of Merioneth, 1576; Canon of S. Asaph, 1602. He resided at Tyddyn Du, in the parish of Maentwrog.

The official seal of the Archdeaconry of Merioneth is now in the Ashmolean Museum, in Oxford. The Curator writes: "The seal is mentioned in our Catalogue for 1836: but I do not know how the seal came to Oxford. It is made of bone." The late Archdeacon Newcome, however, in an article on the subject in the *Archæologia Cambrensis* for January, 1847, p. 19, says this seal is made of box-wood. It is $1\frac{3}{4}$ inches long, by $1\frac{1}{4}$ inches wide. It represents the Trinity: the Father sitting on the Throne, and the Son, in cruciform posture, between his knees; and the Holy Spirit, in the form of a dove, proceeding from the mouth of the First Person. Underneath is a skull decorated with laurels, signifying Victory over Death. The Latin inscription around the seal is, "✠S✠ARCHID ✠DE✠MERION✠" *i. e.* "The Seal of the Archdeacon of Merioneth."

Edmund Prys—a household word in Wales unto this day—was one of the most eminent of Welsh poets; a large proportion of his poetical works is preserved in manuscript. Among these are fifty-four controversial poems—literary controversy was then carried on in poetry and not in prose—between him and William Cynwal, who is said to have fallen a victim to the poignancy of the Archdeacon's satire.[1] The last poem of the series is a pathetic Elegy written by the Archdeacon, when he heard of the death of his rival.[2] At the advanced age of eighty, the Archdeacon wrote some elegant Latin verses in commendation of Dr. John Davies' Welsh Grammar, published in 1621,[3] which contain also some friendly criticisms of Dr. John Dafydd Rhys and Dr. John Davies—two learned Welsh grammarians. The following translated extracts from the Latin verses are interesting.

> " Two sons of Fame with ev'y science fraught
>   (One taught at Sens,[4] and one at Oxford[5] taught)
>   Exert their skill our language to restore,
>   That used by bards in golden days of yore :
>   Both these are Doctors and alike in name
>   (The same their proper, and their sur- the same)
>   In Cambrian tongue both knowing, blest with skill
>   The critic's chair with Dignity to fill.
>   Physicians both—both friends of human kind—
>   One heals corporeal ills, and one the sickly mind.
>   Each in his branch a fair proficience shows,
>   To each his country warm affection owes."

---

[1] Goronwy Owen speaks of Cynwal as the greater genius of the two ; but lacking the education of the Archdeacon he was as unequally matched as one unarmed, untrained, attacking a skilled soldier in full armour.

[2] *Eminent Welshmen*, p. 415.

[3] In his Preface to the work Dr. Davies says he had devoted the leisure of more than thirty years to the study of his native language.

[4] Dr. John Dafydd Rhys.

[5] Dr. John Davies.

K

Of Dr. John Dafydd Rhys, the Archdeacon speaks—

"Tho' Cambrian-born, yet conversant abroad :
The first, by daring Novelty unaw'd,
Attempts our ancient Alphabet to change,
Our vet'ran Troops beneath new Banners range ;
Still in his mind our language holds a place,
Tho' unacquainted with its parent race ;
His native tongue is ever at his heart.
Tho' not well-skill'd in its poetic art,
Whence he blind guides implicitly obeys,
Still pressing on, unconscious that he strays :[1]
Th' attempt we honour, and transmit to fame,
We venerate his love, and glory in his name."

Of Dr. John Davies of Mallwyd, our poet speaks in higher terms of praise—

"But in the last, tho' ne'er abroad, we find
A more attentive, more discerning mind.
Each deep recess of language he explores ;
Nor rests below, but to the summit soars ;[2]
His much loved Cambrians he conducts and brings
By paths direct to Salem's sacred springs,
Points out each stream on Greicia's learned shore,
And bids them drink where he had drank before.
Error's dark night, which erst evolv'd our Isle
(Too long the Dupe of Rome's enslaving Guile),
He lends us light at once to chase away,
And of fair Truth restore the Golden Day.

---

[1] These two lines have reference to Dr. Rhys' explanation and illustration of the Welsh metres and their concatenations, in his Grammar. The Archdeacon was evidently no friend of the "mesurau caethion."

[2] Wood thus speaks of Dr. Davies : "Being well versed in the history and antiquities of his own nation, and in the Greek and Hebrew languages, a most exact critic, an indefatigable searcher into ancient scripts, and well acquainted with curious and rare authors."

He gladly deigns his countrymen to teach,
By well-weighed Rules the Rudiments of Speech,
That when the Root, first, of our own we gain
The Hebrew Tongue we thence may soon attain ;
That, still desirous to improve our Days,
We, blessing God in Cambria's native lays,
May to the Saviour live, to whom be endless praise."

The Archdeacon died in 1624, and was buried, according to local tradition, "before the altar" in Maentwrog Church. It was the custom of the times to bury dignitaries in churches before the altar. As Archdeacon of Merioneth, Prys was connected with Bangor Cathedral, and had a stall in the choir on the Dean's right. More care appears to have been taken in Bangor than S. Asaph to mark the graves of those buried within the Cathedral walls. This neglect accounts for the absence of every trace of Bishop Morgan's grave at S. Asaph. But neither the Church of Maentwrog, nor the Cathedral of Bangor hold an inscription to the memory of Archdeacon Prys. There is a wooden bedstead at Gerddi Bluog, his birthplace, with the letters " E. P.," supposed to have been cut into the panels by himself. His sermon case is now in the possession of the Rector of Llandysul, from which we may infer that the Archdeacon adopted the then common custom of reading his sermons.

Dr. Richard Vaughan, the last of the helpers mentioned by Morgan, was a native of Duffryn, Lleyn, Carnarvonshire. Educated at S. John's College, Cambridge, of which he was a Fellow ; consecrated Bishop of Bangor, Jan. 25, 1595 ; translated to Chester, 1597, and to London in 1604. He died March 30, 1607, and was buried at S. Paul's,

Cathedral in Bishop Kemp's Chapel. He was a distinguished preacher, " a worthy housekeeper, and a liberal-minded man, as the proof did manifest while he lived at Chester, whereunto he was translated. He was an excellent and a rare scholar, a discreet and temperate man, and very industrious in his vocation, which shortened his days. He was translated from Chester to London by King James, in whose grace and favour he lived as any other Bishop whatsoever. He dyed a poor man, for he respected a good name more than wealth."[1] Fuller writes of him : " He was a very corpulent man, but spiritually minded ; an excellent preacher and pious liver. He was a most pleasant man in discourse, especially at his table, maintaining that truth : 'at meals be glad, for sin be sad,' as indeed he was a mortified man. Let me add, nothing could tempt him to betray the rights of the Church to sacrilegious hands, not sparing sharply to reprove some of his own order on that account. He died much lamented."

His cousin, Henry Rowlands, Dean of Bangor, succeeded him in the Bishopric of Bangor, in 1598. A pious and charitable man. He re-roofed the Cathedral at his own expense ; presented five bells ; founded Bottwnog Grammar School ; two Fellowships at Jesus College, Oxford, and Almshouses at Bangor. Bishop Rowlands erected a monument in the Cathedral to the memory of his cousin, Bishop Vaughan, as well as of himself, in the form of two effigies in episcopal habit of post-Reformation pattern, placed in an upright position,

[1] John Wyn's *Memoirs*, p. 92.

in the niches in the north and south walls, within the Communion rails.[1]

Morgan and Rowlands were contemporary bishops in North Wales. The latter died in the year 1616, and was buried before the altar in Bangor Cathedral.[2]

[1] These effigies were found during the last restoration (1870) buried in the walls, decapitated, where they had remained, probably, since the Commonwealth. They have been lately placed in the west corner of the north aisle of the Cathedral.

[2] There is a painting of Bishop Rowlands in the dining-room of the Bishop's Palace, Bangor. He wore a moustache and a short pointed beard, after the fashion of the times.

CHAPTER XV.

Morgan among the Poets—Some Contemporary Bards who sang to his Praise—Ieuan Tew Ieuanc—Sion Tudur—"Cywydd" to "Dr. Morgan, Esgob Llanelwy."

THE name of Dr. Morgan is included in a list of Welsh poets contained in a Welsh manuscript in the British Museum, and having the following title: "Enwau y Beirdd, allan o Lyfr mawr Englynion John Jones o Gelli Lyvydy, yn meddiant William Fychan, Ysg.' Cors-y-gedol, 1773. Ysgrifenwyd 1605—1608. Syr Lewis Gethin; Morgan, Esgob Llanelwy," &c. "The names of the Bards, out of the great book of Epigrams by John Jones of Gelli Lyvydy, in the possession of William Fychan, Esq., Cors-y-gedol, 1773. Written 1605—1608. Sir Lewis Gethin; Morgan, Bishop of S. Asaph," &c. An unsuccessful search was made in the Peniarth Library—the most likely place to hold it—for this "Book of Epigrams." If any of Morgan's poetic effusions have come down to us, we have no data to identify them. Contemporary Welsh poets have not, however, been silent on his merits as a pastor, scholar, and divine. Ieuan Tew Ieuanc, an eminent poet of Cydweli, Carmarthenshire, wrote his "Cywydd i'r Dr. Wm. Morgan, yr hwn a gyfieithodd y Bibl i'r iaith

Gymraeg "—" A Poem to Dr. Wm. Morgan, who translated the Bible into the Welsh language "—in the year 1590. This young poet flourished from 1560 to 1590, the year in which he died ; and thus speaks of Morgan—

> " A gair Duw yn egored aeth,
> Yn deg o'i enedigaeth ;
> Duw a enynodd dawn unwaith
> Doctor auhepcor o'n hiaith,
> Yn deg o niwl a'n dug ni,
> Ac i lan y goleuni ;
> Mae Doctor a rhagoriaeth,
> Morgan wych, mab Mair,
>   A'i gwnaeth ;
> Blaenor, gynghor y gangell,
> Bugail yw heb ei well."

This is singing the praises of Morgan in no measured terms, as a sound teacher, "the leader of the counsel of the chancel," "a diligent pastor, unsurpassed." Neither was the Doctor devoid of eloquence, if we rightly understand the following stanza—

> " Piau helpu o'r pulpud,
> Llyna faeth lle 'ni fethodd,
> Llygad Llanrhaead llawn rhodd :
> Ffrwythder ieithoed *ffraeth draethai*
> Ffynon heb no thro na thrai."

Nor did our poet hesitate to predict that Morgan would some day be a bishop—

> " Doctor i gael rhagor rodd
> Yw y gwr a'i hagorodd :
> *Esgob a fydd ddydd a ddaw.*"

Sion Tudur, in his early days a chorister in S. Asaph Cathedral, Registrar of the Diocesan Ecclesi-

astical Court, and an eminent Welsh poet, wrote a
" Cywydd i'r Doctor Morgan, Esgob Llanelwy "—
" A Poem to Dr. Morgan, Bishop of S. Asaph."—
He graduated as "Dysgybl Pencerdd" at the
Caerwys Eisteddfod in 1568. Tudur resided at
Wigfair, near the city, and was for about two
years a neighbour of the Bishop at S. Asaph.
The following oft-quoted lines form part of this
celebrated poem—

> " Cai glod o fyfyrdod fawr,
> A da dylych hyd elawr,
> Tra gwneir tai, tra caner tant,
> Tra fo Cymro'n cau amrant."

Our poet formed a true estimate of the unbroken
continuity of Morgan's fame, through long ages
then unborn, and which have now passed away.
We, in this age, can appreciate and emphasize his
sentiments, as to the past, present, and future
eminence of Morgan's name in the annals of Welsh
Church history.

Our bard was evidently an old man when he
wrote this poem, for he speaks of himself as—

> " Hen fardd, e fu hardd fy hynt,
> Wyf, a hynaf o honynt,
> Fy mryd yn fy mro ydyw,
> Derfyn f' oes tra fwu'n fyw : "

and he then expresses his earnest desire to end
his days continuing in the chancel of S. Asaph
Cathedral, listening to the reading of Bishop
Morgan's Bible—

> " Tarrio 'nghansel Llanelwy,
> Heb allu myn'd i bell mwy,
> A chanlyn gair, iawn air oedd,
> Darllen yn ffel, byd elawr
> I bobl y mwth y Bibl mawr."

Clearly, the Welsh Bible was read to the cottagers of S. Asaph in the chancel of the cathedral, where it was probably chained in some convenient place, and from which Bishop Morgan himself often read and expounded, in the words of the bard, "i bobl y mwth (or pobl y bwthynod) y Bibl mawr"—"to the cottagers the great Bible." It was ordered by the Act of 1563 that the Welsh Bible should "remain in such convenient places, that such as understood it may resort at all convenient times, to read and peruse the same." The nave of the cathedral was not, it appears, furnished in Morgan's time ; so the Welsh people congregated in the chancel, as Sion Tudur tells us—the most convenient place—to hear the great Bishop "speak in their own tongue the wonderful works of God," and through which the tones of his voice re-echoed, as he read and expounded to them from his own translation of Holy Writ.

About the year 1593 our poet addressed a Poem to Dean (afterwards Bishop) Rowlands of Bangor, soliciting his influence to secure for him a load of slates from the Penrhyn Quarries. Of the Dean he speaks—

> " Deon a'r côr dyn i'r call
> Doctor yn Mangor mwyn gall
> Deon ail sydd Deiniol Sant
> Dwg y traul Dr. Rolant."

Of the house he had built, which lacked a roof, Tudur sang—

> " Ty a wnaeth, mae tô yn ol,
> A gyru a wnaeth gywrain wedd,
> I chwi anerch i Wynedd,
> Toi mawr rhaid ty Meiriadog,
> Symudliw glas medlai glog
> Ceir hir y meistr a'i medd."

We infer from the following lines that slate roofs were being introduced in Bishop Morgan's time, as substitutes for thatched roofs—

"I newyddhau y neuadd hon
Rhwydd y daw rhodd y Deon,
Cer tô gwellt i wr teg ach,
Ysglatus y sy' glytach,
To sy' deg i dy o stad
Teils rhyddion tly'sa rhoddiad
I'w siam-berau ais am brig."

Sion Tudur died in 1602, about two years before Bishop Morgan. In his official capacity of registrar, he knew the Bishop well, and saw him often on business, and was one of his many admirers.

CHAPTER XVI.

On the State of the Welsh Language and its Literature—Influence
of the Welsh Bible on the Welsh Language—The Bible treasured
by the Welsh People—The Language generally spoken at this
Time—Morgan's Defence of the Work of Translation—The Welsh
Gentry unfriendly to the Work—Morrus Cyffin—Dr. Gruffydd
Roberts and Archdeacon Prys on the Opposition to the Welsh
Language in their Time—The Attitude of the Welsh Aristocracy
towards the Welsh Language—Shakspeare and the Welsh—The
poet Spenser and Welsh History—Morrus Cyffin's Welsh Trans-
lation of Jewell's *Apology*—Cyffin on the Welsh Language—His
Notes on Morgan's Translation of the Bible—Dr. John Dafydd
Rhys—His Welsh Grammar—Introduction to the Welsh Gram-
mar—Remarks on the State of Welsh Literature of the Period
—His Desire to improve Welsh Literature—Mathew Arnold and
Edward Freeman on the Welsh Language.

DR. MORGAN'S translation of the Bible was the
legacy of the Reformation to Wales. From a
literary point of view it enriched and fixed the
diction of the Welsh language. The Welsh Bible
has since become, for all practical purposes, the
dictionary of the Welshman. It is *the* one book
of his library; its words, sentences, and principles
have taken deep root in his mind and affection.
The many Bethels, Bethesdas, Calvaries, Zions,
Moriahs and Horebs of the principality show how
thoroughly saturated with Biblical literature the
Welsh mind is. In its moral and religious influences the Bible is pre-eminent in the Welsh

home ; the sick man is afraid to die without *the* Book within his reach ; its prayers and its psalms are known by heart to thousands of young and old. Welsh hymnology—which, for simplicity and deep pathos, is almost unrivalled—is saturated with its language and principles. The Welsh Bible has made the most illiterate peasant more familiar with the history, habits, customs, and geography of the Holy Land, than with the localities of his own native Wales. Many a Welsh peasant knows much more of Zion, Moriah, Carmel, and Calvary, than he does of Snowdon, Cader Idris, Carnedd Llewelyn, and Carnedd Ddafydd. Welsh people who know little or nothing of the Lake District, or of the Rhine, are at home on the Lake of Gennesareth and the River Jordan. Many a Welsh peasant, who has scarcely ever been outside the boundary of his own parish, never seen London, knows every spot in the Jerusalem of the Bible. Men who know nothing of architecture can tell you of the pattern of the temple. All this has given a tone and colouring to the post-Reformation literature of Wales, which has been, almost exclusively, from the time of Bishop Morgan to the present, in the hands of the middle and lower classes. To have been the excavator of the channel through which the blessings of an open Bible, in a language understanded of the masses, have so abundantly flowed, is the highest of all honours any man—be he king or peasant—can aspire or attain to on this earth of ours.

To William Morgan belongs that honour in an eminent degree. His name stands in the same relation to the Welsh language as the name of

Shakspeare does to the English. The former, by his translation of the Bible, infused new life into Welsh literature; the latter, by his plays, did the same service to English literature. Latin was then the language of the learned and polite, and of all public documents in England, and the one employed by numerous writers—Bishop Morgan among them, as may be seen in his Latin dedication of his translation. Evidence of the same thing still exists in the old monumental Latin inscriptions in our churches, while the grave-stones have English inscriptions. The English language occupies a similar position in Wales now as the Latin did in England in Morgan's time. Monumental inscriptions inside the churches of Wales are in English—representing the upper classes; while the tomb-stones have, for the most part, Welsh inscriptions. The only bit of Welsh inscription within Bangor Cathedral is an epitaph to the memory of the priest-poet Goronwy Owen.

The most convincing proof that the Welsh language was commonly spoken in Morgan's time is the fact, that the friends and the foes of the Reformation made such extensive use of it as the most effectual means of reaching and influencing the masses. The paucity of Welsh books in the sixteenth century, as compared to the present state of Welsh literature of every kind, provokes a smile. But it must be remembered that the process of printing was then a very different thing to what it is now, with all our modern improvements, steam appliances and abundance and variety of type, which did not exist when Morgan superintended the passing of his translation through the press. The printing off of each sheet was a slow process, and the work was not put into a stereotype form once for all, striking off any number of copies. Morgan's translation passed through one edition only, and continued in use thirty-two years—the only edition of any kind from 1588 to 1620, when it was revised by Parry. But what was this edition among so many? one copy in each parish church in Wales, and barely even that! The wear and tear of thirty-two years had made them almost unreadable, so Bishop Parry tells us![1] The vast majority of the Welsh people were unable to read then, though they spoke the Welsh language generally. The language must have drawn its existence from some source other than the Welsh Bible, even after its publication. The mere publishing of 800 copies was no life-giving power whatever, at the time, to the Welsh language. No; the seeds of its life were in itself!

There were not wanting in Morgan's time, men who were of opinion that the translation of the Bible into Welsh was a mistake; and the translator experienced considerable opposition to the work on the ground that the Welsh Bible would tend to prolong the existence of the language, and form a barrier to the union of the English and Welsh peoples. The experience of the last three hundred years proves the need of a Welsh Bible, and the wisdom and the foresight of Morgan's action all through. His arguments, in the Dedication, in defence of the work are Scriptural, and consistent with the modern practice of translating the Scriptures into various languages. On the day of

[1] Dedication of 1620 Welsh Bible.

Pentecost this principle was clearly laid down by
Apostolic practice, guided by the Holy Spirit, when
there were in Jerusalem devout Jews out of every
nation under heaven, and "every man heard the
Apostles speak in his own language" (Acts ii. 6). It
would have added to the difficulty of preaching the
Gospel in Apostolic times; and, humanly speaking,
retarded its progress, had the language of the
Apostles been limited to that in which it was
originally written. Morgan had Scripture, reason,
Apostolic and modern practice on his side, whatever may be said of the policy of "worldly wisdom"
against which he battled successfully. Though no
systematic attempt appears to have been made in
his time to crush out the Welsh language, a feeling
evidently existed that it should die, and that the
people should be taught in English or not taught
at all. To this cruel policy the Doctor adds a
timely warning lest the pursuit of it should drive
away all sense of religion from among the Welsh
people. Love of the Welsh language, like the love
of everything else, is not a subject of reasoning
but of feeling, and there are therefore no common
principles by which one can persuade another
concerning it. Whenever that all-wise and over-
ruling Providence ordains, if it does ordain, that
the language shall die, its most ardent lover must
submit to the inevitable. But let it die, if it is to
die, a natural and an honourable death. Let the
parish church be the place where it shall breathe
its last, laying down its hoary head, full of years
and honour, on its Welsh Bible—the pillar which
has supported so many thousands, from age to age,
in the dark valley of the shadow of death—a

befitting legacy to be consigned among the relics of the, it may be, dead languages of the future. With the experiences of the past, the facts and figures of the present respecting the vitality of the Welsh language, he would be a bold man to venture to predict the date of its death. It may die. But the present generation will die ages before it.

Born and bred among the common people, and, as a parish priest, living and moving among them, Vicar Morgan well knew the practical needs of his country. The result of that experience, and of his insight into the character of his countrymen, was a close application of ten years to translating the Bible into the Welsh language. The ground into which the good seed of the Word was cast, was ready to receive it; as its subsequent growth, and the abundant fruit it bore, amply testify.

Morrus Cyffin, a contemporary of Bishop Morgan, thus speaks of the opposition to the translation of the Bible—

"A clergyman from Wales, at an Eisteddfod when mention was made of giving permission to print Welsh, said it was not right to allow any kind of printing in the Welsh language; but he would have the people learn English and lose their Welsh, remarking further that the Welsh Bible would do no good but much harm. . . . . Could the devil himself say better? But who does not know how impossible it is to bring all the people to learn English, and to lose their Welsh, and how deplorable that innumerable souls should be lost."

Dr. Gruffydd Roberts, writing in 1584 in the *Drych Gristionogol*, says—

"You will find some as soon as they see the river Severn or the church steeples of Shrewsbury, and hear an

Englishman say in his language 'good morrow,' who will begin to forget their Welsh and speak much in broken language : their Welsh is Anglicised, and their English, God knows, is too Welshy."

Archdeacon Prys speaks much in the same strain.

"The Welsh gentry," he says, "had by this time formed such associations with England, that their national customs had worn away to a great extent. . . Prejudice was entertained against the Welsh language, and means were adopted, though ineffectual, to abolish it altogether, as a channel too barbarous for their refined machinery of speech."

These extracts show that the objections then urged against the language are identical with those of our own time. The difference between the great mass of Welshmen in Dr. Morgan's time and the Welshmen of to-day, consists in the fact that three hundred years ago they were monoglot, now they are, to a great extent, bi-lingual. The population of Wales is much larger now than it was at the close of the sixteenth century ; and the Welsh and English languages are spoken by larger numbers in Wales now, than was the case in Dr. Morgan's time. It seems strange that as the Welsh were now in favour at Court, the aristocracy of Wales should have assumed a hostile attitude towards the old language. Their ignorance of it probably explains the fact. The poet Spenser, who flourished in Morgan's time, studied Welsh history, traditions, and character; and his favourable representation of them was doubtless acceptable in high places. In Book I. Canto 9, of his *Faërie Queen*, our poet places the scene of King Arthur's home at the foot

L

of the Aran, in Merionethshire, and makes Arthur speak thus of his foster-father, Timon, or Gai, who is supposed to have lived at Caergai—

> "His dwelling is low in a valley greene,
> Under the foot of Rauran mossy hore."

If Spenser ever visited the scene of the subject of his muse, near the source of the historic river Dee, his knowledge of Welsh, if he possessed any before, did not improve thereby. Had he submitted his Welsh orthography to Morgan, Prys, or Cyffin, they would have corrected " Rauran " to " Yr Aran " —the mountain at the foot of which Arthur is traditionally said to have been brought up.

Shakspeare, too, was a courtier, and has done the Welsh character the honour of an introduction into his plays.

Of the model Welsh writers of the period, the name of Morrus Cyffin stands foremost. His translation of Jewell's *Apology* into Welsh, published in 1595,[1] is remarkable for its elegant and pure idiomatic diction ; and, for style, has not been surpassed by any subsequent writer. To the English reader, the following translated extracts from his Introduction to the translation of the *Apology*, are historically interesting, as throwing light on the actual state of things, in his time, with respect to the language and its literature ; while the bi-lingual reader will find an additional interest, and appreciate the style of the writer, in the original extract in the foot-note on p. 166.

[1] This *Apology* was republished in 1671 by Charles Edwards, of Rhyd-y-Croesau ; in 1808 by Rev. Thos. Charles, of Bala ; and has been recently reprinted by the Society for Promoting Christian Knowledge.

"Here is for thee and the good of thy soul, in this book, the substance and summary of the *True Catholic Faith ;* to train and perfect thee in the path of the service of God, and the salvation of man. In reading this thou shalt know the history, and understand the truth of the Christian religion, and with that an exhibition and revelation of the impurity of the faith of the Pope of Rome. May the most High God grant thee to eschew the evil, and pursue the good."

Speaking of the style of Welsh which he adopted, the translator continues—

"I thought it best to set aside the old Welsh words which have become obsolete and not in general use, and I chose the easiest, freest and most readable words I could find, so as to make the style of expression easy, and without obstacle to such as only know the Welsh which is now used."

From this we may infer that Morrus Cyffin put into literature the colloquial Welsh of the period. And he has done his work well, as the subsequent re-issues of his translation amply testify. The translation of the *Apology* is more homely in its style than Dr. Morgan's translation of the Bible ; but the latter is more classical and learned.

After saying that in order to make the translation more intelligible he had, where the Welsh language was defective, imported English, French, Italian, Spanish and Greek words. Cyffin continues—

"And as to the Latin words, who is there that does not know that the Welsh language is nothing more than half Latin throughout? I could if I had time make a book of considerable size of the Welsh words used, which have been borrowed not only from the Latin and the

French, but from the Italian and the Spanish languages also; to say nothing of the Greek, the Hebrew, and such like. It is the ignorant and the foolish that say that these languages have borrowed from the Welsh, and not the Welsh from them. It is useless to argue with such real fools, but leave them in their ignorance and idle talk."

Once more—

"With regard to myself," he continues, "I can say that although I spent most of my life far away [1] from the land of Wales, yet though I was among strange languages, and my time and study occupied with other things, still my greatest care has been to study and keep in remembrance the Welsh language above all others: desiring to be of some good to the language and to the country wherein I was born,[2] according to the doctrine of Plato, the great teacher and the prince of philosophers of deep learning, who said, 'Ortus nostri partem Patria, partem Parentes vendicant, partem Amici'; which being translated is, 'Our birth we owe partly to our country, partly to our fathers and mothers, and partly to the men that we love.' God knows that it would have been much easier for me, and added more honour to my name, to write in another language other than the Welsh. But I see that all things in all languages of belief, are so vigorous

---

[1] The writer of the article on Cyffin, in *Enwogion y Ffydd*, vol. i. p. 90, suggests that our translator may have been an ambassador in one of the foreign Courts.

[2] Morrus Cyffin was the second son of Richard Cyffin, Esq., of Glasgoed, in the parish of Llansilin, Denbighshire, where his family had been settled for many generations. In his younger days he translated the *Andria* of Terence into English. (*Eminent Welshmen*, p. 270.) The family name of Cyffin is derived, according to some people, from the Welsh word cyffiniau, *i. e.* confines, and from their connection with a parish on the confines of England, as Llansilin is.

and pure, through the learning and industry of good men, that they need not (on that account) more. On the other hand, I can scarcely see anything (except the Word of God only in Welsh) of any virtuous fruit in it, to teach and guide the ignorant."

Morrus Cyffin, like Morgan, undertook this work of translating the *Apology* from a genuine love for the spiritual welfare of his countrymen, and the furtherance of the cause of the Reformation in Wales; prompted by the deplorable want of wholesome literature in the vernacular. His words are a serious reflection on the character of the Welsh clergy of the period, who " lived," as he tells, " on the value of men's souls," without paying any regard to the spiritual wants of their flock. It was not mere love of the Welsh language that prompted this pious and patriotic Welshman to engage in this labour of love, but the higher principle of reaching the masses and influencing them for good through the most effectual means, even their own tongue.

Once more. Hear what Cyffin has to tell us of Dr. Morgan's translation of the Welsh Bible, and its influence for good.

" It was Dr. William Morgan that translated the Welsh Bible, late in point of time ; a necessary, heroic, godly, and learned work ; for which Welshmen can never thank him as much as he deserves. Before this it is easy to see how languid the state of the Welsh language was, when scarcely anything was heard but either a wanton song, or some other form of frivolous jeering, without learning, grace or substance in it. If by chance some bard, some time, should endeavour to spin coarsely a little theology in verse, he was deficient in many respects for want of

learning and knowledge, pointing out to the people some
old fable, or old women's stories of the neighbourhood;
and those taken (for the most part) from the book of the
lying monks, called Legenda Aurea, and which may be
called the Treatise of Lies.[1]   I have in my possession a
fragment of such a Welsh song to show, and I am very
sorry in my heart to think that many a soul of man has
been deceived and ruined by means of such terrible folly.
The New Testament was translated in the eighth or ninth
year of the reign of our Lady Queen Elizabeth, but the
printed expressions in it were so largely affected (llediaith)
and incorrectly rendered, that the ear of a pure Welshman
could not bear to hear them read.   It was in this Testament that I saw a godly and learned letter to the Welsh
people from the Right Reverend Father Richard, Bishop
of St. David's, to lead them to know the old catholic
faith and the light of the Gospel of Christ: which letter
the said Bishop wrote in clear, clever, and skilful Welsh,
and doubtless it did much good to every Welshman that
read it." [2]

---

[1] This was no doubt *Bucheddau y Saint,* or the *Lives of
the Saints.*   It was published from Welsh MSS. at Llan-
ymddyfri in 1853, at the cost of the Welsh MSS. Society, in a
royal octavo volume, price £1 1s.   The work is valuable only
for the insight it gives into the state of the Welsh language
in the middle ages, and the great superstition which characterized the Romish teachers of Wales in that period.

[2] The original is as follows, and will serve as a specimen
of Cyffin's style of Welsh composition—

" Dr. William Morgan a gyfieithodd y Beibl trwydo yn hwyr
o amser; gwaith angenrheidiol, gorchestol, duwiol, dyscedig;
am yr hwn ni ddichon Cymry fyth dalu a diolch iddo gymaint
ag a haeddodd ef.   Cyn hynny hawdd yw gweled may digon
llesg oed gyflwr yr iaith Gymraeg, pryd na cheid clywed
fynnychaf, ond y naill ai cerdd faswedd, ai ynte rhyw fath
arall ar wawd ofer heb na dysc, na dawn, na deunydd yndi.
O damweinie i ryw brydydd, ryw amser, geisio bras nyddu y
chydig dduwioldeb ar gerdd, ef a balle mewn llawer pwnc

So wrote Cyffin of the excellencies of Morgan's work, and of the inefficiency of Salesbury's translation.

A learned contribution to Welsh literature, and the only one through which the learned of foreign countries can form any accurate estimate of the metrical properties of the Welsh language of this period, was from the pen of one of the most eminent Welshmen of the century, Dr. John Dafydd Rhys, a native of Llanfaethlu, Anglesey, where he was born in 1534. Through the assistance of Sir William Griffith of that parish, Rhys was enabled to enter Christ Church, Oxford, from whence he removed to Sienna, in Tuscany, where he studied medicine, and took the degree of Doctor of Physic at that famous University, and became a perfect master of the Italian language. It was in 1592 that he published, through the London

---

eisieu dysc, a gwybodaeth ; gan hynodi i'r bobl ryw hen chwedl, neu goel gwrach ar gwir y barth; a hynny wedi ei dynny allan (y rhan fwyaf) oolyfr y Myneich celwydog, yr hwn. a elwid *Legenda Aurea*, ag a ellir ei alw *Traethawd y Celwyddeu* Y mae 'n fy meddiant i beth o'r fath gerdd Gymraec i'w dangos, ag y mae yn dostur iawn gan fy nghalon i feddwol ddarfod twyllo ag anrheithio llawer enaid dyn drwy y fath erchyll ynfydrwydd. E ddarfuasid cyfieithu'r Testament newyd ynghylch yr wytbfed neu'r nowfed flwyddyn o Deyrnas eyn barglwydes frenhines Elizabeth, ond yr oedd cyfled llediaith a chymanit anghyfraith yn yr ymadrodd brintiedig, na alle clust gwir Gymro ddioddef clywed mo' naw'n iawn. Yn nhal y Testament hwnnw y gwelais i lythur duwiol dyscedig at y Cymry, o waith y gwir barchedig Dâd Richard Escob Meniw, i'u twyso nhwy i adnewddiad yr hen ffydd gatholic a goleuni Efengyl Crist : yr hwn lythyr a scrifennodd y doededig Escob mewn Cymraec groyw, hyfedr, ymadroddus, a diammeu wneuthur onaw les mawr i bob Cymro a'i darllenodd."

press, the work above referred to, namely, a Latin-Welsh treatise on the Grammar of the Welsh language ;[1] which treated also of the Welsh metres, which he took great pains to explain and illustrate.[2] Dr. John Dafydd Rhys wrote also in Welsh a compendium of Aristotle's *Metaphysics*, which was never printed : the manuscript was, at one time, in the Library of Jesus College, Oxford, but it is now lost. He also wrote, in Italian, a treatise on *The Rules for the obtaining of the Latin Tongue*, which was printed at Venice.

Humphrey Prichard,[3] who wrote a Preface to the Grammar of Dr. Rhys, says that the principal object of the work was to facilitate the better understanding of Dr. Morgan's translation of the

---

[1] There is a copy in Bangor Cathedral Library. The title-page reads: "Cymræca Linguæ Institutiones. J. D. Rhæso Monensi Llanvaethlæo. Camb. Bryt. Medico Senensi Lat. and Welsh, London. T. Onion, 1592." There is also a copy in the Royal Library at Paris.

[2] Dr. Samuel Johnson, in his Notes of his visit to North Wales in 1774, has the following item under Aug. 5th, in the Diary, when he dined with Mr. Myddleton of Gwaenynog. "The table was well supplied, except that the fruit was bad. . . . After dinner, the talk was of preserving the Welsh language. I offered them a scheme. Poor Evan Evans [Ieuan Brydydd Hir] was mentioned as incorrigibly addicted to strong drink. . . . I recommended the republication of David ap Rhees' Welsh Grammar. . . . At Bodfari I heard the second lesson read and the sermon preached in Welsh. . . . The sound of the Welsh, in a continued discourse, is not unpleasant."

[3] He was a native of Bangor. He held the living of Llanbeulan, Anglesey, in 1548, to which he was preferred by Bishop Bulkeley. He was then a Romanist, but in 1570 he subscribed to the XXXIX. Articles before Bishop Robinson of Bangor.

Welsh Bible.   The accuracy of this statement has, however, been questioned, inasmuch as Rhys, at the time of the publication of the Grammar, was a Romanist; there can, however, be no doubt as to his great love of the Welsh language, the study of which he did not neglect; though, like Morrus Cyffin, he had spent most of his life abroad.

His Introduction to the work, addressed " To the noblemen, gentlemen, bards, lovers of the Welsh language, and others of my beloved country-men of the nation of the Cymry, and to all others who may read this work, greeting, and wishing them all health and prosperity," is of historic interest, bearing on the state of the Welsh language and its literature at that time.

" There is scarcely one language in all Europe and its islands, as far as I have been able to discover," says Dr. Rhys, "which has not from time to time been cultivated and improved by the scholars and inhabitants of those countries, except the ancient Welsh, our own mother-tongue, which now of late has received some little cultivation and improve-ment from some few learned and good men of the present age ; and that principally for the purpose of translating the Bible into our own language. For if we look about us, and examine what has been the conduct of other nations, such as the Greeks and Romans, we shall find that there is scarcely any learning or knowledge, any art or science, which has been discovered by man, that has not appeared in their books and been published to the world ; so that all Europe is full of their learned works, and the authors thereof not only celebrated, but immortalized through all ages.

And next to these, if we survey the other nations of Europe in general, such as the Italians, the Spaniards, the French, the Germans, the English, the Scotch, and many others which might be mentioned, all of whom have paid particular attention to their native languages; and their learned men have so far cultivated and improved them, that there is scarcely one of them that does not contain all the learning, information and knowledge, and all the arts and sciences, for which the two nations before mentioned are so celebrated. And the books published by these learned men, in their different languages, will not only continue to do them credit, for their assiduity and acquirements, but will also remain as everlasting monuments of the improved taste of those different nations, and their advanced state of civilization."

This testimony is true. The Welsh language has produced no book in philosophy, law, science, or art worth mentioning. Its literature is almost exclusively theological, with a later development into the domain of politics by the multiplication of newspapers and magazines in the vernacular. Dr. Rhys gives the true reason for this lack of variety in Welsh literature, which is not far to seek even in our own time, i. e. the want of cultivation of the language and its utilization by men of culture. The study and the use of the language then, as now, was confined to the middle and lower classes, hence the inferior nature of its literature. Notwithstanding this, the scholarly Welsh translation of the Bible—and Biblical knowledge is the highest of all sciences—has made an impression far more indelible on the masses in Wales than the English Bible has in England, or the various translations of Holy Writ on any class of the community in the whole of Europe. The almost entire absence of scientific and light literature in the language of Wales has not been without its good effects, inasmuch as the Welsh mind has been diverted into one channel of study, i. e. the Bible.

The severe strictures of Dr. Rhys are less applicable now. An appreciable change has taken place, and a desire evinced by the gentry to know the Welsh language, and so strengthen the bond of union between them and the people among whom they live. A revered nobleman—not a Welshman—who resided in Wales for nearly half a century, expressed his regret a short time before his death, because he had not acquired a knowledge of the language when he first took up his residence in Wales, and so avoid the many inadvertent mistakes of his long and useful life. The Doctor's censure is aimed at those of his countrymen who neglected and despised the language of their forefathers. Speaking of his own times, Dr. Rhys says—

"But as for us Welshmen, we may observe that many of our countrymen have become so vain, so proud, so conceited, so affected, and so negligent of everything that is patriotic, and so ignorant of their own language, and so attached to everything that is foreign and exotic, and, consequently, so different from most other nations, that if they have been but a short time out of their country, they pretend to have forgotten their own native language; and, if they condescend to

make an attempt to speak it, they do it in so conceited and affected a manner, that their former
acquaintance are astonished to hear them, and feel
quite ashamed of them; and at the same time that
they affect to despise their own native language,
they take a pride in attempting to speak English,
French, and Italian, or some other foreign tongue,
when at the same time they are but imperfectly
acquainted with those foreign languages, and by
no means capable of conversing in them either
fluently, elegantly, or grammatically. But these
vain, shallow upstarts may be justly considered as
a degenerate race and the outcasts of society; and
those persons who are desirous to abolish and
utterly to extinguish the Welsh language, and to
substitute the English in its place, are deserving of
no better treatment, nor can they be considered as
worthy of any regard, or be held in any higher
estimation: for this, in truth, can never be accomplished without destroying the Welsh nation, and
establishing English colonies."

From the persistently expressed false ideas of a
few—unquestionably ignorant of the real state of
things—it is an interesting and refreshing contrast
to turn to the following candid and enlightened
testimonies.

"To preserve and honour the Welsh language
and literature," writes the late Matthew Arnold, "is
quite compatible with not thwarting or delaying
for a single hour the introduction, so undeniably
useful, of a knowledge of English among all classes
in Wales."

"In truth," writes Professor Freeman,[1] "I suspect

[1] *Archæologia Cambrensis*, Oct. 1876, p. 328.

that we do not always take into account how very
remarkable a phenomenon in European history
the separate existence of the Welsh language
really is.   Even the modern Principality is no
inconsiderable part of the island.   If we add on
those parts of the island which we reckoned as
Welsh within comparatively recent times—Corn-
wall and Strathclyde—it makes a very considerable
part of the island indeed.   Wales as it is, is a
much greater relative part of Britain than Breton-
speaking Brittany is of Gaul, or than the Basque
lands are of Spain.   The existence of that stub-
born British tongue which has survived two con-
quests; the fact that, in spite of the coming of
Claudius and the coming of Hengest, an appreciable part[1] of Britain still speaks the tongue of
Caradoc and Boadicea, is a fact which has no real
parallel in Western Europe."

[1] Mr. E. G. Ravenstein, F.R.G.S., in his work on *The
Geographical Distribution of the Celtic-speaking Population
of the British Isles*, says that the Welsh language is still
spoken by 1,006,100 souls, *i. e.* by nearly five-sixths of the
people of Wales.
   The present circulation of weekly newspapers in the vernacular is said to exceed 120,000 weekly; the monthly circulation of magazines 150,000.   One Welsh publisher has
issued a single work at a cost of £18,000, and profited
thereby; and a Scotch firm has already sold £36,250 worth
of translations into Welsh.   It is estimated that the Welsh
reading public expend £200,000 per annum on literature
published in their native tongue.

PART III.—1595 TO 1604.

CHAPTER XVII.

Morgan Bishop of Llandaff—Consecration and Enthronement—
Entry in Archbishop Whitgift's Register—The Ordinal of 1552
—Welsh Services in the Ladye Chapel of Llandaff Cathedral—
Contemporary Dignitaries—Morgan's Episcopate at Llandaff—
Lambeth Articles—Bishop Morgan's Theological Views.

BY nomination of Elizabeth, at the recommendation of Whitgift, Morgan was appointed to the
Bishopric of Llandaff in 1595, vacant by the translation of Bishop Babington to the see of Exeter,
on February 4, 1594.[1] Morgan's promotion was
expressly a recognition of his work. " The translation (of the Bible) he dedicated with a Latine
Epistle prefixed to Qu. Elizabeth, for which work
he was rewarded with the Bishoprick of Llan-,

---

[1] Wood's *Athen. Oxon.*, vol. i. p. 745 : " Regina, Decano et
Capto Eccliæ Cath. Landaven. Cum Eccliæ predicta per
promotionem Gervasii Babyngton net. Epi. ad Episcopatum
Exon. jam vacet. Licentiam eligendi : T.R. apud Westmon.
xxiii. Julii reg. 37, 1595." (Lansdowne MSS. British
Museum, 938, f. 40 ; Rymer xvi. 278.)
" Regina : cum vacante nuper sede Landaven, per translat.
Gervasii Babington nuper Epi. ad Epatum Exon. Decanus
et Captum, Willielmum Morgan. S.T.P. sibi in Epum
elegerunt Nos Regium Assentum, Mandantes, &c. T.R.
apud Westmon. xii. Jul. reg. 37, 1595." (Ibid. 279.)

daff first, and afterwards with that of St. Asaph" (Wood, *Athen.*, i. col. p. 615; Lansdowne, 983, f. 40, in the British Museum). So he owed his promotion more to himself than to any one else, and was about forty-eight years of age when he entered the Episcopate. His confirmation to the see took place on the 18th July, 1595, in the Church of S. Mary the Virgin, London, before Richard Cosyn, Vicar-General, and in the presence of John Redman and John Coston, Notaries Public. The consecration followed on the 20th[1] of the same month, at the parish church of Croydon, Whitgift being the consecrating prelate, assisted by the Bishops of London (Richard Fletcher), Norwich (William Redman), and Rochester (John Yong). There were also present, Richard Cosin, Dean of Arches; Gabriel Goodman, Dean of Westminster; Martin Fotherby, and Samuel Finch, Vicar of Croydon with others.

The particulars of Dr. Morgan's consecration were duly entered in Whitgift's *Register*, Part 2, f. 55b, now in Lambeth Palace Library. The contents are quite formal and in Latin, having an entry in English that the Service of Consecration used was the " Forme and manner of making and consecrating Bisshopps, Priests and Deacons."

It is historically interesting to note the difference in the words of consecration of the Ordinal of 1552, and the words subsequently introduced. The exact words used by Whitgift in the act of consecrating Morgan were, " Take the holy goste, and remember that thou stirre up the grace of God,

---

[1] " Provectus ad sedem Landavensem an. 1595. Consecratus Julii 20." (*Hist. S. John's Coll. Cambridge*, vol. i. p. 254.)

which is in thee, by imposicion of handes: for God hath not given us the spirite of feare, but of powere, and love, and sobernesse."[1] There is no special reference here to the office of a bishop, and the words are as applicable to a priest or deacon. Morgan had also been ordained deacon and priest according to the 1552 Ordinal. The changes as they now stand in the present Ordinal were made in 1662; "office and work of a Priest" are not in the Ordinal of 1552, but were introduced in 1662. The words "office of a Deacon" are, however, in the Service of 1552 for the ordination of Deacons. But the separate Offices for the consecration of Bishops and ordination of deacons and priests, clearly show the threefold nature of the ministry of the Church of England; and the XXXVIth Article of Religion is quite clear upon the point. The three orders were not as distinctly mentioned in the Litany in Morgan's time as they are now. The petition ran thus in the English and Welsh Prayer-Books: "That it may please thee to illuminate all bisshops, pastours and ministers of the Churche." "Teilyngy o bonot, lewyrchy yr holl Escyp, Bugelydd a gweinidogion yr Eglwys."

Objections have been made to the validity of the consecrations of bishops according to the Ordinal of Edward VI. and Elizabeth—Morgan among them—because of the omission of the words, "for the office of a Bishop." But the whole Service concerns bishops; and there could be no mistake on the part of any one present, that it was episcopal consecration that was conferred. This objection came from a Romish direction; but even

[1] Prayer-Book of 1552.

in the Roman Pontifical, the words which accompany the imposition of hands are simply, "Receive the Holy Ghost"; and the prayer which follows does not directly mention the office of a bishop.

Bishop Morgan was enthroned and put in possession of the temporalities of the see, Aug. 7, 1595.[1] The Ladye Chapel was in Bishop Morgan's time set apart for Welsh services, at which he himself often officiated. The Chapter consisted then of fourteen members, viz. the Bishop, acting as Dean—there was then no Dean of Llandaff—Archdeacon Morgan Nicholas—1595 to 1601—and twelve prebendaries. The names of those who occupied the stalls in Morgan's time are given in Browne Willis' *Survey of Llandaff Cathedral.* Evan Morgan, the Bishop's nephew, was Precentor from 1595 to 1601.

Cardiff was then, as now, the market town of Llandaff. But it only comprised a number of mean streets; the greater portion of the town was within the walls, Crockherbtown, or, as Speed calls it, Cokkerton, was the only part of Cardiff outside the walls. The town possessed ships then, which carried on a trade in coal with Bristol and other seaports. Neath was then considered the best place for ship-building. All the Welsh towns were, at this time, very small and insignificant; but they were attractions to the wealthy and rich during the winter months, whence they resorted from

[1] "Breve Reginæ Escaetori suo, de restit. temp. Willielmo Morgan S.T.P. Landaven. electo. T. R. apud Westmon. vii. Aug. reg. 37, 1595." (Rymer xvi. 280; in Lansdowne 983 f. 40, British Museum.)

their country seats, for recreation and enjoyment. The leading gentry possessed houses in the chief towns, some of which still exist at Chester, Carnarvon, and Brecon. The municipal offices were generally held by them ; the democratic element, which now so largely exists in towns, was not felt much in Morgan's time. With a limited franchise, political power was in the hands of the few. The Welsh people laboured under many disadvantages; being for the most part ignorant of English, and far removed from the metropolis, they were little acquainted with what was going on in the outside world.

Of the six years of Bishop Morgan's episcopate at Llandaff there is but little to record. He had designed great things for that diocese—and was only prevented from carrying them out by his translation to S. Asaph—one being the erection of an episcopal palace.[1] The Bishop's castle, before it was destroyed by Owain Glyndwr, stood on the south-east of the cathedral, and was a stately building, as the ruins of the gateway indicate. The see, too, had been greatly impoverished by the avarice of more than one of his predecessors, by the leasing and letting of church property, insomuch that Godwin, Morgan's successor, charges Kitchin with having almost ruined it.

In the very year of Morgan's consecration, the Lambeth Articles were put forward. The predestinarian controversy, which began at Cambridge, excited great attention, rapidly extending itself far beyond the limits of that university. The sympathy which had sprung up between the English

[1] Lansdowne (British Museum) 983, f. 40.

and Calvinistic reformers on the continent, made the teaching of the former more in harmony with the Calvinists. Convocation never approved of the Lambeth Articles, and they were, therefore, never embodied in the formularies of the Church of England. Bishop Morgan was probably at the Lambeth Conference in 1595. In the battle which from 1564 to 1604 the Church rulers were waging against the Puritans, Morgan was doubtless on the side of Whitgift, of whose administration he speaks in unmeasured terms of praise. "The most Reverend Father in Christ, the Archbishop of Canterbury, that most excellent Patron of literature, most keen champion of the truth, and most prudent guardian of order and seemliness."

CHAPTER XVIII.

TRANSLATION OF BISHOP MORGAN TO S. ASAPH, 1601—1604.

DEAN OF S. ASAPH, THOMAS BANKS, M.A., 1587—1634.

Morgan's Translation to S. Asaph—Arms of the See—Presides at a Chapter Meeting—Constitution of the Chapter—The Cathedral of S. Asaph—Restores the Chancel of the Cathedral—Dean Banks—Morgan holds a Synod of his Clergy—The Convocation of 1603—Archdeacon Prys Canon of S. Asaph.

ON the death of his friend and patron, Bishop Hughes, October 1600,[1] Bishop Morgan was, by the express desire of the Queen, translated from Llandaff to the then more lucrative see of S. Asaph.

He was the forty-fifth bishop of S. Asaph, from the foundation of the see ; and the fourth bishop in the Reformation line.

The subject of the arms of the see of S. Asaph has been a long-disputed question. Bishop Morgan adopted the " Key on Crozier," as the Episcopal seal attached to the subsidy in the Record Office testifies. Some of his predecessors adopted the Cross Keys. The earliest known impression of the arms of S. Asaph—1433-44—has " Key on

[1] Browne Willis' *Survey of St. Asaph Cathedral*, vol. i. p. 107.

Crozier." Every bishop whose seal is at the British Museum, and assumed armorial bearings, charged the dexter side with the arms of the see. Bishop Hughes assumed the other arms of the see: dexter, two Keys endorsed in saltire; his family arms on the sinister. Bishop Parry, Morgan's successor, adopted the Key on Crozier as the arms of the see on the dexter, Lion passant on a Bend on the sinister, as his private coat. Bishop Parry also adopted the open Book in chief after Bishop Morgan—probably as the reviser of the Welsh Bible.

Speed's map of Flintshire (1610) gives a bird's-eye view of the county of Flint, the cathedral and city of S. Asaph, together with the episcopal palace of Bishop Morgan's time.

Although Morgan was not elected by the Chapter of S. Asaph till July 12, 1601, nor enthroned in the cathedral till September 21 in the same year, he presided at a Chapter meeting held at S. Asaph on March 8, 1601, "pro concionibus habendis in Ecclesia Cathedrali Assaphensi."[1] The following scheme was agreed upon at this Chapter, as to the number of sermons to be preached at the cathedral annually, by the respective members of the Chapter. The Dean, six sermons; the Archdeacon (*i.e.* the Bishop, for the Archdeaconry was then attached to the bishopric) six; the Prebendary of Vaenol, five; of Meliden, five; the Comportioners of Llanfair, eight; Prebendary of Meifod, three; each of the Canons, two; and the Lord Bishop on Ascension Day, All Souls, Christmas Day, and Good Friday.

The Chapter of S. Asaph, at that time, consisted

[1] Browne Willis' *Survey*, vol. ii. App. lxi. p. 149.

of the Archdeacon of S. Asaph (*i. e.* the Bishop himself); six Prebendaries, and eight Canons Cursal with stalls in the choir of the cathedral. The choir, as described by Browne Willis, in 1720,[1] was probably much the same in Morgan's time. On the stalls are inscribed Prebend: Vaynol, &c. The Canons and Vicars-choral take place according to seniority. The choir up to the altar was well floored with freestone, intermixed with grave-stones.[2] The stalls handsomely wrought, and there was a large canopy, or arch, over each of them, with carved pyramids at top about four feet high; and over all, through the whole length of the stall was a plain canopy of wainscot; so that the height of the stalls and canopy over them was about fifteen feet, said to have been built in the time and at the charge of Bishop Redman, 1471—1496. From beyond the stalls up to the altar, and also round the altar, the wall was covered with wainscot well finished with Belection work, which was painted, as were also the stalls. The plan shows the present position of the stalls in the choir. But until the renovation at the beginning of this century they all stood in the chancel, where the stalls probably occupied the same relative position to one another.

The benefices which were held *in commendam* by his predecessor, Bishop Morgan released, thus sacrificing income. Following the example of his brother and neighbour, Bishop Rowlands[3] of Bangor,

---

[1] *Survey*, vol. i. p. 15.
[2] Among these was the grave-stone of Bishop Morgan.
[3] He re-roofed the nave of Bangor Cathedral at his own charges.

though lacking his private means, Morgan "repaired and slated," at his own expense, the chancel of S. Asaph Cathedral, then in great ruin.[1] This was due partly to the avarice of some of his predecessors, who had stripped the roof of the cathedral, sold the lead, and allowed the fabric to fall into ruin. Morgan "slated the roof,"[2] being probably too poor to replace the lead. The slates were, most likely, procured from the Penrhyn quarries; for we find Sion Tudur, in 1593, soliciting the help of Dean Rowlands of Bangor, to procure slates for him to roof a house at S. Asaph. Thomas Banks, the then Dean of S. Asaph, who held the Deanery from 1587 to 1634, appears to have taken no interest in the Cathedral building. He died at Talar, in the house belonging to the Deanery, and was buried on the south side of the Cathedral. The "Discouerie of the present estate of the Bishopprick of S. Asaph" has the following account of him. "The Deane . . . . one banks not 23 *years old*.[3] He that now hath the name to be Deane nev^r kepte house in all his lief. And is an unfitt man for that place & callinge in all respects, being not past xxiiij yeres olde." Dean Banks survived Bishop Morgan thirty years.

As the Psalmist of old took pleasure in the stones, and favoured the dust of Zion, so also Bishop Morgan had pleasure in restoring the ruined stones of the mother-church of the diocese over which, in the good providence of God, he had been called to preside. No wonder that, like Nehemiah

[1] *Memoirs*, by Sir John Wyn, p. 96.
[2] *Ibid.* p. 96.
[3] *I.e.* when this complaint was made, in 1587.

of old, the good Bishop's countenance was sad to see God's house, the resting-place of the dust of so many fathers-in-God, almost laid waste. A true reformer, and a wise leader, he practically proved his motto to be, "Let us rise up and build."

On the 20th October, 1601, within a month of his enthronement, Bishop Morgan held a synod of his clergy at S. Asaph; the record of which supplies the number and order of Sunday and week-day services.

The diocese of S. Asaph was represented in the Convocation of 1603-4, at which the "Constitutions and Canons Ecclesiastical" were drawn up and agreed upon. Morgan, probably, took part in the deliberations of that assembly.

Soon after he came to S. Asaph, Bishop Morgan gave his old friend, Archdeacon Edmund Prys, a canonry in the cathedral, vacant by the death of Rice Wynne, Rector of Eglwysfach. The stall the Archdeacon held was that of "Arthur Bulkeley," Canonia Secunda, of the then annual value of £2 6s. 8d. He was installed October 8, 1602.[1] Though the canonry was not of much pecuniary value, it was a recognition of the help the Bishop had received from the Archdeacon in the work of translation. "Edmund Prys," the name by which he is familiarly known to this day, was sixty-one years of age when he became a cursal canon.[2] He survived his friend and patron twenty years. According to a note by W. Morris, on a copy of Moses Williams' *Repertorium Poeticum*,

[1] Browne Willis' *Survey*, vol. i. p. 282.
[2] Cur-sal, *i. e.* Cursales. In most cathedrals they are called Honorary Canons, but Cursal Canons at S. Asaph.

now in the British Museum, Archdeacon Prys died
in 1623, aged eighty: "Edmund Prys, obiit 1623
yn 80 oed, person ffestiniog a Maentwrog, ac arch-
diacon Meirionydd. Claddwydd dan yr allor yn,
Eglwys Maentwrog"—"Edmund Prys, died 1623
aged 80, the parson of Ffestiniog and Maentwrog,
and Archdeacon of Merioneth. He was buried
under the altar in Maentwrog Church." This agrees
with the local tradition respecting the place of
burial; but there is no inscription to his memory
anywhere. In the hexameter Latin verses which
the Archdeacon wrote in 1621, he says, "Rescriptum
Edmundi Prysæi, Senis Octogenarii Archdiaconi
Meirion in Approbationem Operis." Here the
Archdeacon testifies that he was eighty years old
in 1621, and therefore eighty-two at his death in
1623. This makes him two years older than the
age given on the manuscript in the British Museum.

CHAPTER XIX.

A.D. 1602.

Clerical Subsidy in the Public Record Office bearing Bishop Morgan's Autograph Signature—Geographical Division of S. Asaph Diocese—Identification of Bishop Morgan's official Seal attached to the Subsidy.

THERE is in the Public Record Office a Clerical Subsidy, written in Latin, and dated 1602, bearing the signature and official seal of Bishop Morgan. From this document we gather that the diocese of S. Asaph was then divided into seven rural deaneries, viz. (1) Rose (Denbigh); (2) Mold; (3) Queenehope (Hope); (4) Marchia (Oswestry); (5) Pola (Pool); (6) Mowthwy, or Mowddwy. This part of Merionethshire was then in the diocese of S. Asaph, including Machynlleth, so that Dr. Davies, of Mallwyd, was one of Bishop Morgan's clergy. By a comparatively recent exchange of deaneries, Mowddwy, with Cyfeiliog, have been transferred to Bangor diocese; and the Vale of Clwyd Deanery transferred from Bangor to S. Asaph diocese. It is remarkable that this deanery should have been in Bangor diocese, when it is geographically in the heart of the diocese of S. Asaph. All the territory from Ruthin down to Corwen was under the supervision of the Bishop of

Bangor, during, and for a long time after, the time of Bishop Morgan.   This accounts for the absence of any reference to that part of the county of Denbigh in the Subsidy.   (7) Penllyn and Edeyrnion.   This is the only portion of Merionethshire which is now in the diocese of S. Asaph.   The Return is meagre as an index to all the parishes in the several rural deaneries.

The official seal of Bishop Morgan, with the impression of his signet ring on the reverse side, attached to this document, is so worn down that it is difficult to determine whether the figure in chief be an "open Book," or the Welsh harp.   Morgan, like all bishops of that period, signed his name in Latin ; thus—"Willm̄ : Asaphen " ; and, to judge from his autograph on this subsidy, wrote a more readable hand than many of his contemporaries. He followed the fashion of the times of adding an elaborate scroll to his signature.   The device on the official seal represents Jacob blessing Ephraim and Manasseh, with crossed hands, one over each head, and is copied from the seal of John White, Bishop of Winchester 1556, which has the names " Ephraim," &c., by the figures.   The seal has a legend round it nearly obliterated, which is, as far as can be made out : " Sigillum Episcopale Guillermi Morgan Asaphensis " ; while the date 1601 is quite clear.   At the foot are the arms of the see, on the dexter side of the shield, with the arms of Bishop Morgan on the sinister side.

CHAPTER XX.

AMES I. 1603—1625.

ARCHBISHOPS OF CANTERBURY.

JOHN WHITGIFT, 1583—1604.
RICHARD BANCROFT, 1604—1611.
GEORGE ABBOTT, 1611—1633.

BISHOPS OF S. ASAPH.	*BISHOPS OF BANGOR.*
WILLIAM MORGAN, 1601—1604	HENRY ROWLANDS, 1598—1616
RICHARD PARRY, 1604—1624	LEWIS BAYLY, 1616—1632
JOHN HANMER, 1624—1629	

BISHOPS OF S. DAVID'S.	*BISHOPS OF LLANDAFF.*
ANTHONY RUDD, 1594—1615	FRANCIS GODWIN, 1601—1618
RICHARD MILBOURNE, 1615—1621	GEORGE CARLETON, 1618—1619
	THEOPHILUS FIELD, 1619—1627
WILLIAM LAUD, 1621—1627	

Accession of James I.—The Millenary Petition—John Wyn of Gwydir and the Gunpowder Plot—Dr. Thomas Williams of Trefriw.

BISHOP MORGAN lived to see the accession of James I. All religious parties sought the King's patronage; but he soon showed that he intended to govern on the same lines as Elizabeth had done. The Puritans presented the Millenary Petition, in which they pleaded for a revision of the liturgy;

in consequence of which James summoned a conference at Hampton Court in 1604. There is no record what, if any, part Bishop Morgan took in this Conference ; he appears to have led a studious life, and to have abstained from engaging in the theological controversies of the times. Baker, in his *History of S. John's College*, aptly sums up Morgan's life and labours thus : " uno opere dedit omnia."

James had, in return for the peaceful acquiescence of the Romanists in his accession, promised that the penal statutes of Elizabeth against them should not be enforced ; but he found public opinion in England far too strong against Romanism to allow him to abolish them. For remitting the fines imposed on Recusants,[1] he was accused of fraternizing with Romanists, and there was such a large influx of Jesuits into the kingdom about this time, that the word went abroad that James had been received into the Church of Rome. At last the King was obliged to enforce the recusancy fines, and banish Roman priests out of the country. The " Gunpowder Plot " arose out of this.

John Wyn of Gwydir, who was member of Parliament for Carnarvonshire at the time of the Gunpowder Plot, was dissuaded from going up to the opening of Parliament on the notable 5th of November 1605, by Dr. Thomas Williams of Trefriw, a Romanist, who came to him just as he

---

[1] This is a French name derived from the Latin *re*, against, and *causa* a cause, and was applied to those Romanists who refused to obey the Elizabethan Act of Uniformity. They were subject to heavy fines for not attending their parish church on Sundays and holy-days.

was setting out for London, and earnestly entreated him not to go that session, from which it is inferred that Williams knew something of the plot. Bishop Humphreys relates this on the authority of a state-ment he received from his father, who had heard it from Lady Bodvel, Sir John Wyn's daughter.

Dr. Thomas Williams was educated at Brazenose College, Oxford, where he graduated M.A. in 1573. He took to the study of medicine, and practised that profession at Trefriw. He wrote a book of Welsh Pedigrees, entitled, *Prif Achau holl Gymru Benbaladr*, in which he states that he began the work in 1578, enlarged it in 1585, and added much to it in 1609. It was never printed, more than any of his other works. But the greatest of all his works, as regards merit and labour, was his *Lexicon Latino-Britannicum*, or Latin and Welsh Dictionary, which shows great research ; and is valuable more particularly for its copious extracts from manuscript authorities. Williams, in his *Dictionary of Eminent Welshmen*, p. 537, says that the abridgment of the work professed to be given by Dr. Davies is little better than a bare index, and that he had had an opportunity of comparing them. His patron and kinsman, Sir John Wyn of Gwydir, in a letter dated October 21, 1620, suggests a plan to Dr. Williams by which he might publish his dictionary ; but the terms seem to have been unsatisfactory, " For," he says, " the Latin and Cambrian Diction-arie, which with greate laboure and travayle, as God knoweth, I have congested and digested these fiftie years, I see very small surtie or consideration for my paynes, and therefore I mean not in haste, God reward you for your permission, to deliver the same to any of these men, whose great promises I have tried to small effect, in things done for them, and imparting certaine collections unto them, never receiving quid pro quo for any of them. God doth know that in the four years while I did write the Dictionaries, I was so instant to the work that often when I came from the book, I did not know many time what day of the week it was, and soe lost my practis that might have been a hundred pounds unto me or some great matter, and during that time I have pined for hunger, yf it hath not been for God and your worships good considerations and not to these illiberal men's liberalities." The original work, in the author's handwriting, is now in the Hengwrt Collection at the Peniarth Library, and forms three quarto volumes. The title-page bears the dates of 1604 and 1608 ; and appears to have been completed in the latter year. In the same collection are other manuscripts by the same author; among them " Llyfr Prophwy-doliaethau Cymraeg a Saesonaeg a Lladin o law Sir Thomas Williams "—" A Book of Welsh and English and Latin Prophecies from the hand of Sir Thomas Williams."   He also compiled a pretty large Herbal, in Latin, Welsh, and English, giving an account of herbs and their medical virtues.[1]

[1] Williams' *Dictionary of Eminent Welshmen*, p. 528.

CHAPTER XXI.

A.D. 1603.

The Controversy between Bishop Morgan and Mr.[1] John Wyn of Gwydir[2]—The Correspondence.

THE last years of Bishop Morgan's life were not passed in peace. The bitter controversy between the good Bishop and his powerful neighbour, John Wyn of Gwydir, is said to have hastened the Bishop's death. Be that as it may, his letters do honour to his name and memory, for his keen sense of justice, and his unflinching defence of the rights of the Church, against the machinations of his unscrupulous and avaricious opponent.

The dispute arose out of a refusal, on the part of the Bishop, to grant John Wyn a lease of the tithes of the rectory of Llanrwst, and which roused the bitter indignation of the Squire of Gwydir. Bishop Morgan had himself shown a spirit of commendable self-sacrifice in waiving his right to the benefices held by his predecessor with the bishopric. And, as he points out in the correspondence, it would have been an act of gross injustice to lease Church property under its value,

---

[1] He was created Baronet in 1611.
[2] Gwydir, from Gŵy, aqua, and Tir, terra ; the lands being much subject to the overflow of the Conway.

for the personal gain of any man. Much scandal and loss had been caused to the Church by the action of some of Morgan's predecessors in this respect. His stern resistance proved that he was true to himself, and to the Church. The character of such a man commands respect. Such unflinching firmness, and, at the same time, Christian kindness, are invaluable qualities where, in the high and arduous office of a bishop, sensitiveness would be a superfluity. Bishop Morgan was an iron commander, who did not shrink from the conscientious discharge of his duty, for the dread of incurring the displeasure of the socially most powerful personage in his diocese—as no doubt John Wyn was.

" His character has been held up as all that was worthy, and decried as everything that was crafty. He was member of Parliament for the county of Carnarvon in 1596; one of the Council of the Marches of Wales; and created a baronet in 1611. Being shrewd and successful in his dealings, people were led to believe he oppressed them; and ' it is the superstition of Llanrwst to this day, that the spirit of the old gentleman lies under the great waterfall, Rhaiadr y Wennol,[1] there to be punished, purged, spouted upon, and purified from the foul deeds done in his days of nature.' It is recorded that in 1615, Sir John having incurred the displeasure of the Council of the Marches, Lord Ellesmere, the Chancellor, was appealed to; but the 'shrewd' baronet made his peace

---

[1] A corruption of Rhaiadr ewynol (*i.e.* the foaming falls). It has nothing to do with wennol, swallow. The original and the translation—swallow waterfalls—give a wrong impression of the meaning. ("Samaria, ei brenhin a dorrir ymaith fel ewyn ar wyneb y dwfr."—Hos. x. 7.)

N

in the surest manner, by paying a bribe of £350. He was a man, evidently, who tried to make the best of both worlds; for after squaring the court with his bribe, and managing to keep his name on the Commission for Carnarvonshire, he made his peace with heaven by founding a hospital, endowing a school at Llanrwst, and giving up sundry tithes to support these charities."[1]

Such was the character of the man—no ordinary one—with whom Bishop Morgan entered into conflict. John Wyn had wealth and power on his side. No one visiting Llanrwst now, even at this distance of time, can fail to see lasting memorials of him all round, especially in the parish church; reminding us of the once great name which was impressed on all this region. Bishop Morgan had no nobility but the nobility of earnestness, and no credentials but the priesthood of the truth and the power of the right. The Bishop's weapons of warfare were not carnal, but mighty through God to the pulling down of strongholds; as the following correspondence[2] testifies.

"Salutem in Chro.
        "Youre motyves that I shold confyrme Your Lease upon the Rectorye of Llanrwst are dyverse, vz.
    "1. Your greeffe to mysse, havynge neaver fayled before of anie attempte.
    "2. That you had rather forgoo £100 landes a yeare.
    "3. That the rent reserved ys as much as the Rectorye ys worth.
    "4. That youe purchased the Lease deere.
    "5. That ye world may thynke youre love to me warde unkyndlye rewarded.

---

[1] *Memorials*, p. vii.
[2] See Appendix (p. 137) to Yorke's *Royal Tribes of Wales*.

" 6. That others, by my example, wyll lesse esteme youe.

" 7. That youe hope to finde me such to youe, as youe are to me.

" 8. That the adjoynyng of Tybrith did cost you much.

" 9. My sundrie promysses that youre Lease shold be the fyrst. And one thynge moveth me agaynst all these, vz. my conscience, wch assureth me that youre request ys such, that in grauntyng yt I shold prove my selfe an unhonest, unconscionable and irreligiouse man; youe a sacrilegiouse robber of my church, a perfydiouse spoyler of my Diocesse, and an unnaturall hyndrer of preachers and good scholers;—the consyderatione whereof wold be a contynual terror and torment to my conscience. And to com to youre motyve reasons :

" 1. I pray God that youre greeffe of myssynge be not Achab's greeffe for Nabothe's vineard.

" 2. 100£ landes are worth 200£. tyth.

" 3. I credyblie heare that Rectorye to be worth twyse the rent reserved ; the wch youre seconde reason confyrmeth.

" 4. Youre 4 reason confyrmeth the same ; for you would not purchase deere a Lease worth lytle more then the rent.

" 5. Youe have shewed to me much kyndnesse, but no unhonest kyndnesse ; neather do I ever meane to denie youe in youre honest requestes.

" 6. Youe shall not be the bett r estemed by gettynge ungodleye requestes, but worse thought of; for to fayle of badd attemptes ys no shame, but to relynquysh them wylbe greate credyt.

" 7. Youe shall finde me, such as I desyre to finde youe, in omnibus licitis et honestis, youre assured.

" 8. I do not counte the adjoynyng of Tybrith to be eather hurtfull or beneficiall to me or the church.

" 9. My promysse was and ys, that I wyll do nothing

for anie subject wch I wyll nott do for youe, and that I wyll not confyrme anie such Lease as youre's before youre's. Neather am I nowe mynded to confyrme anie lease at all. But the Chaptre do meane to revyve one lyff in a lease of theare's.

"Amongest other youre kyndnesses, youe gave good testymonie of me. I pray youe lette me continewe worthie of it. So manie chypps have bene allreadye taken from the church, that yt ys readye to fall. God hath blessed youe so well, that youe are bounde rather to helpe hys poore church then to hynder yt.

"Thus wth my hartiest commendationes to youre selfe and good Mystres Wyn, I reast

"Eveare youre owne in ye Lorde,
"WILLM. ASAPHEN.
"Verte folium.

"15° Ffeb^r
1603.

"I knowe of syxe or seaven suters for confyrmationes of Leases upon presentatyve benefyces, wch meane to brynge the landes of Pryvye Counsellers, yffe not Hys Majestye's owne lande. And at the next Parlament, I look to be layde to. But I trust y^t God wyll defende me and hys church.

"W. A.

"One wold open the doore for all the reaste.
"To the Right Wor. his
veary lovying Frend, John
Wyn of Gwedur, Esquier."

This letter reminds one of John the Baptist's rebuke of Herod, a rebuke which cost him his life; and of S. Paul's gentle remonstrance, "I am not mad, most noble Festus; but speak forth the words of truth and soberness." The selection of the figures of S. John the Baptist, S. Paul, and S. Peter, in Bishop Morgan's memorial window in the parish church of Penmachno, is singularly appropriate—a graceful tribute to the character of the man whom it commemorates.

Mr. Wyn replied—

"Hominibus ingratis loquimini, lapides. The sower went out to sowe; and some of his seede fell in stonie ground, where hitt wythered, because hitt could take no roote. The seede was good, but the land nought. I may justly say soe by you. I have in all shewed my selfe your ffreinde, in soe much as yf I had not pointed you the waye with my· finger (whereof I have yett good testimonye) you had beene styll Vycar of Llanrhayder. You pleade conscience when you should geve, and make no bones to receave curtesie of your ffreinds. But I appeale to him that searcheth the conscience of all men, whether you have used me well, and whether hitt be conscience (wch you ever have in your mouth) be the sole hinderance of my request. I wyll avowe and justiffie hitt befor the greatest Dyvyns in England, that it hath beene, now ys, and ever wylbe, that a man may wth a salfe conscience be farmour of a lyvinge, payeing in effect for the same as much as hitt ys woorth; and so ys this, surmyse you the value to be as you layst. Nether was the losse of the thynge that I regard a dodkyn, but your unkinde dealinge. Hitt shall leson me to expect no sweete fruite of a sower stocke. Your verball love I esteeme as nothinge; and I make noe doubt (wth God's good favour) to lyve to be able to pleasure you, as much as you shall me, et é contrá. You byd me thanke God for his many benefytts towards me. God graunt me the grace ever soe to doe. In truth, I did much thanke Him in mynde to see you preferred to the place you are in, as yf you had beene my owne brother; but that I recall, for I never expect good wyll of you, nor good torne by you.

                    "JOHN WYN,

"Gwyder, the house that   "of Gwyder.
did you and yours good,
   24th February, 1603.

"To the Reverend Father, The
Lord Busshop of St. Asaphe."

This letter does not deal with the question at issue, and is a curious mixture of piety and insolence, personality and recrimination. Mr. Wyn gives himself undue credit when he claims to have been the means of promoting Morgan to a bishopric. With reference to this, the Bishop writes to Mr. Martyn, a mutual friend, to whom Mr. Wyn appealed to mediate between them in this dispute—

"He [Mr. Wyn] wrote unto me allreadye, that yff he had not bene, I had contynued yet Vicar of Llan Rhayadr. How much he ys deceaved herein, youe and others do knowe. But yff I had contynued Vicar of Llan Rhayadr, I had bene in better case then nowe I am. I had testimonials inough bysydes that wch he procured; and I had prevayled, yff I had none, as my Lo. of Canterburye and my L. Treasurer beleved. Yet I confesse that Mr. Wyn thearein shewed greate love (as then I thought) to me; but (as now I fynde) to hym selfe, hopynge to make a stave of me to dryve preachers partryges to hys netts."

The probabilities of the case are also strongly corroborative of the Bishop's statement. Morgan was chaplain to the Archbishop of Canterbury, and well known in high quarters, where he com-

manded much influence and respect. Mr. Wyn
could not have possessed much, if any, political
influence at the time of Morgan's elevation to
Llandaff in 1595, for he was not returned as member of Parliament for Carnarvonshire till 1596, the
year following. Mr. Wyn, no doubt, exerted all
the influence in his power in Morgan's favour, and
the Bishop acknowledges that "Mr. Wyn shewed
greate love" to him in this matter of the bishopric ; but to assume that he alone was the means of
placing the mitre on Morgan's head, would be to
un lerrate the great work of the Bishop in the
service of his country and his church—the principal factor of all in the influence which seated him
on an episcopal throne ; to depreciate the percep-
tion of higher powers, and conceding to Mr. Wyn
an amount of influence which he never, at any
period of his life, actually possessed. Whatever
kindness Morgan received—and they were many, as
he himself admits—he was not indebted to him,
to any appreciable extent, for his elevation to the
bishopric of Llandaff, nor for his subsequent
translation to S. Asaph.

Bishop Morgan does not appear to have answered
this letter of the 24th February, 1603. On the 13th
March, in the same year, the Squire of Gwydir
wrote to Mr. Martyn, to "complaen of my L. of
St. Assaphe."

"Mr. Martyn.
      "Sir,
           "No greefe to the greefe of unkyndness :
They rewarded me yll for good to the great dyscomfort
of my sole. I may say so, and justly complaen unto
you of my L. of St Asaphe, who (besydes what hys

ancestors receved by myen) ys dyversly, and in great matters, behouldynge unto me, whereof (beynge schooled by hys late letter, of wch I send you a trew coppy) thoghe I expect no rent, yett yt easethe my wronged mynd muche, to lay open hys hard dealyngs towards me, and my benefyts towards hym, befor you, who are not ignorant that I delyver but a truethe, in most of them havynge been an eye Wytnes.

"Hyt squarethe therfor wth a good method in a narration to begyn wth my deserts, wch I will run over breefly ; wch I wold have you to put hym in mynd of : 1. in that he protested to hys late servant Tho. Vaghan, that he remembered no more thereof, then that I had lent hym my geldyngs to go to Llandaff, and had sent hym a fatt oxe att hys fyrst comynge to St Assaphe. W^{ch} ys to strayne a gnatt, and swallow a camell.

"Fyrst, I let hym have a lease uppon hys farme of Wybernant,[1] part of the township of Doluthelan for forty years, for forty poundes in money. The farme he hathe sett att the yerly rent of twenty foure poundes per ann: and yeldethe of the Kyng's rent viii s. too pence yerly, as farre as I remember.

"In measurynge the sayd farme wth my farme of Penannen, I let hym have, in Pant yr Helygloyn, land to the valew of iij£ yerly; for wch my Uncle Owen Wyn reprooved me muche.[2]

"I bare the hatred of Ieuan M^r dythe, and his nephew Ed. Morice, the lawyer, durynge his lyfe; for

---

[1] Bishop Morgan's birthplace.

[2] Assuming that Mr. Wyn had let this farm below its value, which is very doubtful, that was a matter for his own consideration, and concerned no one else, as it was his own private property. But Bishop Morgan did not stand in the same relation to Church property, though his power over it was absolute. He was a trustee, and far too conscientious a man to take advantage of his legal powers, to repay any real or supposed personal favours, at the expense of the Church.

that I was a daysman, and agaenst hym; I mean, Ieuan M^r dythe, and appointed my frends commyssyoners agaenst hym.

"Was hyt not I that first delt wth Mr Boyer to make hym Bushopp, and made the bargen, S^r? Mr Boyer was nether knowen to hym, nor he to Mr Boyer; ergo, yf that had not beene, he had contynued styll Vycar of Llan Rhayder. I know you do not forgett what was objected against hym and hys wyf to stopp his last translation, and how that my certyfycatt and my frends quitted hym of that imputation, and so made hym pre-vayle; for the wh^ch both they and I wear worse thoght of by those we have good cause hyghly to respect.

"I labored, as yf hit had beene to save the lyf of on of my chyldren, to end the cause of dylapidations between hym and my coosin Dd. Holland; knowynge hit wold have beene his great hynderance to be so matched att first dashe. How sufficyent a man, how well ffrended, and what a tootheman in hys suets my cousin Holland ys, every man that knowethe hym, knowethe that also.

"My L. of St Assaphe I knew to be but poore (hys translation havynge stood him in muche) yett wylfule and heddy to run into law suets;[1] therefor I was as muche trobled to reclaeme hym to reson and consyderation of his owen estate as I was to bringe the adversse part to reson and conformyty. My L. Bushopp's cheefe lyvynge was the tenthe of the Paryshe of Abergele,

---

[1] These law suits were unavoidable to defend Church property against the designs of worldly men. It would have cost the Bishop less trouble had he not moved at all. But he felt his responsibilities too keenly to be a passive observer of the robbing of the Church. He bore the expenses of defending her rights. The Bishop did not dispose of any Church property to defray the costs of "defending his poor church," as Bishop Bulkeley of Bangor, under similar circumstances, did before this.

where my coosin Holland comandeth absolutely. Yf they had gone to suet of law, he would have so wronged hym in the gatherynge of the tythe, as hit shold have beene lyttell worthe unto hym. My self excepted, was ther on Jent. in the contrey wold once have shewed hym self for hym agaenst my coosin Holland? and that knew he well. But my L. can make use of Jent. when they serve hys torne, and after decarde them upon pretence of conscyence; wch may appere by the coppye of his letter unto me, whereof, I avowe on my credyt this ys the trew coppye. This much touchynge that matter of my desert; and now touchynge my request.

"Mr Sharp, my L. Chancelor's chaplen, beynge by hys L. collated parson of Llanrŵst, leased hys benefyce to on Robt Gwyn of Chester, who appointed a ffrend of myen, on Robt Vaughan, brother to my brother Tho. Vaughan, his under farmor. Doctor Elice,[1] somtyme a great comander in theese quarters, in favor of Doctor Meryke (who rewarded him wth a township of teythe whear his manyson[2] house was in 'Spytty) dyd geeve lev to dysmember the parsonadge of Llanrŵst of Tybrithe tythe, and to joine hit to Corwen. Whear-uppon, pyttyinge to see Llanrŵst churche dysmembered by unlawfull practyse, acqueanted my L. of St Assaphe, that I meant to stand for the right of Llanrŵst agaenst Doctor Meryke, wth an intent to do more for that churche, as I then made knowen to my L.[3] The suet

---

[1] Dr. Elis Price.

[2] Plas Iolyn, Yspytty.

[3] This action of Mr. Wyn, in defending the rights of Llanrwst church by an action at law, is hardly consistent with blaming Bishop Morgan for defending the rights of the whole diocese in the same way. They were, however, prompted to the same process of defence by different motives. Mr. Wyn by a selfish greed of obtaining the emoluments of the benefice, and the Bishop by a deep sense of duty to his church and clergy.

prooved, by Dr Meryke's weywardnes and hope in his fautors, more chardgeable and troblesom then was expected. Whereuppon I eftsons acquainted my L. Bushop, that I ment to buy Robt Gwyn's lease into my hands, that, surrendringe hit, Mr Sharp (in consyderation of my great chardge in the suet) myght grant me a lease of the lyvynge for iij lyves, the only mean in som part to quit my chardge;[1] wch he promysed me to confyrme, and that hit should be the fyrst of all other that should receve confyrmation. Havynge to my chardge and troble compassed Robt Gwyn's lease of 10 years, and by surrender of the same gott a new lease of three lyves of Mr Sharp, I sent hyt to be shewed my Lord by my servant Wm Lloyd; who then seemed to myslyke hit, and answered doubtfully touchynge the confyrmation, wth all chidd Mr Sharp in souche sort, as givynge cause to have my lease new made, he made me pay 10 £ more then was att fyrst, by reson my L. Bushop had chidd hym. In end, hearynge of a Chapter appointed for the confyrmation of the other leases, I sent myen also by my son Mostyn, and my letter to my L. the contents whearof you shall fynd in my Lord's answer. To wch I

---

[1] Mr. Wyn was a shrewd man of business. Having been bitten in the lawsuit, he sought to obtain the costs from the profits of a lease on the benefice. This really explains the whole dispute between him and the Bishop. "The adjoyning of Tybrith," which was the point on which Mr. Wyn went to law, the Bishop says he did "not counte eather hurtfull or beneficiall to me or the Church" (see point 8 in his letter to Mr. Wyn, p. 195), that is to say, the church in the diocese would not suffer by the transfer of the tithes of Tybrith from the benefice of Llanrwst to that of Corwen. But it would have made all the difference in the world to Mr. Wyn, because, in the event of a lease being granted, Llanrwst would be of so much less value. It is, therefore, quite clear that Mr. Wyn cared more for defending his own interests than for the rights of the Church.

receved this answer, wch whether hit be fyttynge my desert ys your's to judge, as also to expostulat with hym, beynge oure ffrend, common to us bothe.

"I am not of nature to put up wronge; for as I have studied for hys good, and wrought the same, so lett my L. be assured of me as bytter an enemye (yf he dryve me to hit) as ever I was a stedfast frend; nether ys he com to that heyght, or wantethe enemyes, that he may sey, *Major sum, quam cui possit fortuna nocere.* For as *Honores mutant mores,* so *mores mutant honores.* I am ashamed for hym, that he hathe geeven herby cause to his enemyes and myen to descant of his ungrate dysposition ever aggravated towards hym. Hys answer at lardge I pray you retorne me, yf nothynge els.

"Your lovynge ffrend,

"JOHN WYN,

"of Gwyder.

"Gwyder, this xiijth of Marshe, 1603.

"He promysed me an advowson of the levynge by Tho. Roberts, when he denyed the confyrmation. I sent unto hym the same man, w^thin too dayes after for the same, and my coosin Elice Vaghan w^thall; and he denyed me eny, sayinge he had provyded no preferment for his wife, and that he myght overlyve Sharpe,[1] and have that lyvynge in comendam. So to conclude, I must have nothynge but a scornefull, chetynge letter, in leu of all my good indeavors."

If this letter lacks argument, the writer of it was evidently not wanting in arrogance and self-esteem. Mr. Wyn was mistaken if he meant, by means of threats, to force the Bishop to a compliance with his request. Bishop Morgan was possessed of two keen a sense of justice, too strong a will, and the

---

[1] Peter Sharp, D.D., was rector of Llanrwst from 1602 to 1616.

undaunted courage of a true man, to shrink from a conscientious discharge of what he believed in his inmost heart to be his duty in this, to him, painful difference between himself and an old friend and neighbour. Undeterred by the threatening attitude of the Squire of Gwydir, and the total shipwreck of an old friendship, the Bishop sent to Mr. Martyn the following calm, firm, and forcible response.

"Salutem in Chro.

"I fynd that Mr Wyn hath acquaynted you wth the unkyndnes wch he conceaveth in me; and I am glad to have so indyfferent an arbytrator. Hys requeste was, that I wold confyrme a Lease for three lyves upon the Rectorye of Llanrwst (being a presentatyve benefyce, fytt to be some preacher's lyvynge) at the yearelye rent of 50£, the thynge being worth 140£, and being of my patronadge. Thys requeste much perplexed my mynde, for that yt grêved me to denye Mr Wyn anye thynge, and my conscyence reclaymed agaynst the grauntynge of thys thynge, being so prejudiciall to preachers, speciallye to the next incumbent and to the churche yt self, wch wanteth competent mayntenance for preachers.

"To com to the pleasures that Mr Wyn dyd unto me, they are not so greate as he accounteth them; for I payd for hys time upon Wybernant, and hys uncle Rob^{te} 40£ or more att one tyme, beinge a greater some then they had of anie of the other tenantes that held lyke landes in that township. I pray God forgeve Mr Wyn hys harde dealynge wth these tenantes, whose tenementes he could not covett wthoute impiety. In measurynge of Pant yr Helygloyn, I had lesse then some affyrmed to be due unto me, and more then others wyshed; in leue whereof I was to erect a stone wall, or a dytch of earth, betweene me and hym to my greate charges.

"Jeuan Meredydd and I weare ffrendes, when, upon

Mr Wyn hys request, I gott to hys brother Robt Wyn his nowe wyf; wch caused such hatred and sutes betwene me and the sayd Jeuan, that yt cost me from 60£ to 100£ more than I had.   Mr Wyn in deed procured to me two commyssioners, Mr Morys Johnes once, and Mr Morys Lewys, an other tyme; and was my daysemen to ende that cause.   I sustayned all those broyles and obloquyes for hys sake and hys brother's.

"He wrote unto me allreadye, that yff he had not bene, I had contynued yet Viccar of Llan Rhayadr. How much he ys deceaved herein, youe and others do knowe.   But yff I had contynued Vicar of Llan Rhayadr, I had bene in better case than nowe I am.   I had testymonials inough bysydes that wch he procured; and I had prevayled, yff I had had none, as my Lo. of Canterburye and my L. Treasurer beleved.   Yet I confesse that Mr Wyn thearein shewed greate love (as then I thought) to me; but (as nowe I fynde) to hym selfe, hopynge to make a stave of me to dryve preachers partryges to hys netts.   I thanke Mr Wyn for his paynes in daynge betwene me and Mr Holande; although he gott me but 150£ wheare I shold have had 1000£. But I may not requyte thys paynes wth the spoyle of anie church.   Yt seemeth that Mr Wyn thynketh that I do but pretend conscyence.   But I assure you, in verbo Sacerdotis, that I think in my harte, that I weare better robb by the hygh waye syde, then do wch he requesteth.   And I knowe that as to serve an errynge conscyence is a falt, so to do agaynst conscyence, though yt be errynge, ys a synne.   Yff my ffathere and mothere weare lyvynge, and made the request that Mr Wyn maketh, I hope that I sholde have the grace to say them nay.   I fynde farther that Mr Wyn is in two errors; the on ys, that I promysed to hym a confyrmatione of that Lease; and the other ys, that I promysed hym by John Robtes an advowson; wheare in truth I

promysed neather of both, but told Mr Wyn that I wold
be veary loath to confyrme anie Lease upon anie presentatyve benefyce; that I wold do for hym as much and
more than anie other; and that yff I wold confyrme anie
such, hys shold be the fyrst.   I neaver confyrmed anie,
nor meane to do.   But the Chapter and I graunted, not
iij lyves, but one lyff, not upon a presentatyve benefyce,
but upon an impropriatione, wch is a dyvydent amongst
manie, and can not be occupyed by anie of us, for that
we are farr of, and thearefore must be letten for one
terme or other; and the incumbe ys for the church, and
not for a lay man.   But Mr Wyn, thoughe he knoweth
that theare ys dyfference betwene grauntynge a lease of
oure owne and confyrmynge the lease of an other man;
betwene a presentatyve benefyce and an impropriatione;
betwene one lyff and iij lyves; betwene a publyke use
and a pryvate, styll exclaymeth, that I have confyrmed a
lyke lease, and wyll not according to promyse confyrme
hys.   My answeare to John Robtes was, that a Bushopp's
advowson wold not bynde the successor; and when he
asked, whyther Mr Wyn shold have yt, yff yt dyd bynde,
I told hym, that, yff yt dyd bynde, he shold have yt and
myne eares also; for that I dyd well knowe that yt can
not bynde.   And when he cam next to aske, yff I wold
graunt yt de bene esse, whyther yt wold bynde or not, I
told hym, I wold not, and that yt was no part òf my
promyse or meanynge.   John Robtes mystooke my
wordes concernynge my wyff; for I dyd not say that she
must be fyrst provyded for by me rather then by such
leases; I wyll not spoyle ye church.   Thys was the
effect of my then speach, whearby Mr Wyn myght have
understoode that nothynge dryveth me to thys resolutione,
but my conscyence.   Of my Commendam, I dyd and do
say, that yff I weare so lewde as to confyrme all the
leases in the Diocesse, yet I wold not be such a foole as
to confyrme anie, before I weare better provyded for

my Commendam. Yff I dẏd, tell Mr Sharpe, that he
shold do well to leave hys lyvynges to hys successors as
ffree as he founde the same. I dyd but my duetye. Yff
thys weare not a case of conscyence, you shold not
neede to perswade me to gratifye Mr Wyn; for hys
owne requeste ys of greate force wth me. Youre two
reasons, or rather hys reasons (for he used the lyke in
hys letters to my selfe) do lytle move me. For yff I
shall fynde hym as bytter an enemye, as ever I founde
hym my frende, yt wylbe a comfort to me to suffer in so
good a cause. I knowe that God, whose church I wolde
defende, ys able to defende me agaynst all énemyes, and
wyll defende me so farr, as he shall see yt to be
expedient for me; that Mr Wyn can not kyll my soule,
nor do to my bodye more then God wyll permytt. And
my confydent trust ys, that God wyll not permytt anie
thynge to be commytted agaynst me, but that wch shalbe
for my good, eather in thys worlde or in the worlde to
com. And yff dyverse men wyll dyversely descant of
thys unkyndnes; What? Ys thys to move á man that
shold be setled in conscyence, to do agaynst conscyence!
I knowe that some do blame me in hys presence, and
blame hym and commende me in his absence. And yt
may be that others do use me in lyke sort. Inconstans
et mutabile vulgus. Auxilium meum in nomine Dni.

"Thus resolved to do neather thys nor anie other act
that shal be prejudiciall to the church,
                    "I rest,
              "Amicus usque ad aras,
                          "WILLM. ASAPHEN.
    "(To Hys very lovynge Frende, Mr.
Thomas Martyn at hys house over
agaynst S. Andrewe's, in Holborne.)"

    "(My L. Bushopp, being in London
at the Parliament, wrote this unto
me. THOMAS MARTYN.)"

So little is known of the story of the Bishop's life, that the preservation of this correspondence is valuable, because it gives posterity an insight into the noble character of the man—his inner life—who gave his country the Bible in the mother tongue. That work is in itself an abiding proof of his learning, industry, and zeal. These letters are a living proof of the Bishop's earnest aspirations, by precept and by example, to act up to the principles of the same Divine Word. The work of translating was not a mere mechanical mental labour, but its principles had taken deep root in the action of his life. "Whatsoever things are true, whatsoever things are honourable, whatsoever things are just, whatsoever things are pure, whatsoever things are lovely, whatsoever things are of good report; if there be any virtue, and if there be any praise, think on these things." Bishop Morgan might have continued the apostolic precept, without inconsistency or presumption—"The things, which ye both learned, and received, and heard, and saw in me, these things do: and the God of peace shall be with you" (Phil. iv. 8, 9).

O

CHAPTER XXII.

A.D. 1604.

Illness, Death and Burial of Bishop Morgan—Amount of Money found in his Purse at the Time of his Death—The Time and Place of Burial—No undue Haste in his Burial—Bishop Parry's Letter to Mr. John Wyn—Mr. Wyn's Pique against Bishop Morgan—Special Commission issued by the Crown to enquire into the State of his Effects—The Furniture—His outdoor Effects—Glimpses of Social Life in Morgan's Time—John Lloyd of Vaenol Fawr and the Bishop's Effects—Bishop Parry.

BISHOP MORGAN did not long survive the controversy. This, with the threat of Mr. Wyn to be as much of an enemy as he had been before a friend, may have lent a colouring to the tradition that it shortened the Bishop's days. The squire of Gwydir was as good as his word. The letter, written by the Bishop a short time before his death, sufficiently proves this, and that he was not in good health, as appears from his signing himself, "Yoᵣ sickly neighbour."

[LETTER FROM BISHOP MORGAN TO MR. JOHN WYN.]

"SALUTEM IN CHRO.

"Seeinge you can better agree wᵗʰ my tithe in Langustenyn then with me, and have, as I heare, taken order for the gatheringe of it; I am loath to contrarie you therin, soe that you send me money by this bearer for the same, although I knowe my tithe to be worthe twise as much as you pay for it. But I pray you to cause the tithe of Bodescallan to be gathered in kind; for yor cosen Hugh Gwynne Gru : hath written to me that he would tithe it in specie this yeare.

"Thus wishinge you in all things the direction of the Holy Ghost, I rest,

"Yo^r sickly neighbour,

"WILLM. ASAPHEN.

"At St Asaph, the 24th July, 1604.

"(To his wors. neighbour, John Wyn of Gwydir, Esquire.)"[1]

Bishop Morgan's personal troubles and minis-terial anxieties remind one of the experiences of a greater than himself—"In perils by mine own countrymen, in perils in the city, . . . in perils among false brethren; in weariness and painful-ness : beside those things that are without, that which cometh upon me daily, the care of all the churches" (2 Cor. xi. 28). Christ triumphs in the hearts of His servants by wrongs meekly borne, even more than by wrongs legally righted.

Bishop Morgan died at the Palace, S. Asaph, on September 10th, 1604, when the autumnal tints showed nature to be hastening with rapid steps to her winter's grave, at the comparatively early age of fifty-seven years—the autumn of life, when the gray hair, and the faded look, are not short of admonishing us that the meridian of life has been passed. "Though he was soon dead, yet fulfilled

---

[1] Yorke's *Royal Tribes*, p. 147.

he much time."[1] "A good life hath but a few days."[2]

Posterity would have liked to know what his last words were as his life was ebbing away; and the names of those gathered around that illustrious death-bed—a forlorn hope at this distance of time. That his wife, if she survived him, watched over the great Bishop with tender care to the end cannot be doubted. And we may naturally suppose that his nephew, Evan Morgan, Vicar of Llanasa, was also there; and probably the domestic chaplain, to administer the consolations of the Church, in the administration of the Holy Sacrament, breaking on the solemn stillness of the dying hour in the "comfortable words" of the Communion of the Sick. That the Word of God was a lantern unto his feet, and a light unto his paths through the Dark Valley of the Shadow of Death, to lead him to "the fulness of joy in God's presence, and pleasures at His right hand for ever more," is as certain as the same Word has since been, and still continues to be, to thousands of his countrymen through the medium of his translation. The then customary "passing bell," probably tolled forth its mournful tones, from the tower of the Cathedral hard by, to tell the parishioners that the spirit of the great Bishop was passing away.

The "Inventorie" of the Bishop's goods, to which we shall refer at greater length presently, contains a list, with a valuation of each article of

[1] Wisdom of Solomon iv. 13.
[2] Ecclesiasticus xli. 13.

furniture " in the chamber where the Bishopp lay,"
as follows :

Two fether beddes	} x. . .^{s}
One boulster	
Two payer of sheetes	x. . .
A white Cadowe	x. . .
A Coverlet	x. . .
A pillowe and a pillowe beere ...	xii$^{[d.]}$
A Curten over the Doore	xi$^{d.}$
A . . . . pott	[v]iii$^{d.}$
A lookinge glasse	xx$^{d.}$
Two brushes	x$^{d.}$
A . . . . [Bedsteed ?] ... .·.	ii$^{s.}$ vi$^{d.}$
A greate Cupborde	xxx$^{s.}$
xliii peeces of pewter of all sortes ...	} xxxiii$^{s.}$ iiii$^{d.}$
Seven pottingers two Candlestickes ...	
Fower Andierns	xi$^{[d.?]}$
Two Flagon pottes	v$^{d.}$

This document breaks upon the almost uniform
vagueness of facts in the history of Bishop Morgan's
life and death. To it we are also indebted for the
information : " Redy money founde in the said
Bishop's purse when he died iiii$^{s.}$ viii$^{d.}$ " Four
shillings and eight pence was not a large sum in a
bishop's purse ! In this, as in other respects,
Bishop Morgan was "a good minister of Jesus
Christ "; yielding almost a literal obedience to the
precept of his Great Master : "provide neither
gold, nor silver, nor brass in your purses." Among
" certen other old appell of the said Bishopps " are
mentioned, " Two ould gounes," and three ould
cassocks," valued at 5s. !
Man's happiness consisteth not in the abundance

of temporal goods, but a moderate portion is sufficient for him. There is none in the world, be he
king or bishop, without some tribulation or per-
plexity. Bishop Morgan tells us he would have
"bene in better case had he contynued Vicar of
Llanrhayadr."

He was buried on the day next after his death,
in the choir of his own cathedral church, without
any inscription or monument.[1] The exact spot
wherein his body was laid to rest, "in sure and
certain hope of the Resurrection to eternal life," is
not known ; but he was probably buried, according
to the custom of the times, like most dignitaries,
before the altar. There is not a stone to his
memory within or without the cathedral. If there
ever was a monument or inscription of any kind
over his grave, not a vestige of it remains. Most
probably the cathedral never held a monument to
Bishop Morgan, his representatives being too poor
to erect one. There was, indeed, a flagstone in
the choir, with the letters "W. M." cut into it,
which was removed during the restoration of 1870,
to make room for the more ornate encaustic tiles
which now adorn the floor of the choir. If this
stone marked the grave of the great Bishop, it
answers literally to the "garreg arw a'r ddwy lyth-
yren" of the Welsh poet's celebrated lines to the
"Poor Man's Grave." A diligent but unsuccessful
search was made for the stone a short time ago.
It was probably used heedlessly for some purpose,
or carried away as *débris*.

The case of Bishop Morgan is not exceptional as

[1] Browne Willis' *Survey of S. Asaph Cathedral*, vol. i.
p. 108.

regards S. Asaph Cathedral, for there is no inscription to the memory of his predecessor and successor in the see. There may have been monuments or inscriptions at one time, demolished during the Commonwealth, as in the case of the monuments of Bishops Vaughan and Rowlands in Bangor Cathedral.

There is no ground for supposing that there was any undue haste—prompted, it is said, by Mr. John Wyn—attending Bishop Morgan's burial. It appears to have been the custom for people to be so buried at that time. Sir John Wyn himself was buried the very next day after his death.[1] So that it could have been no mark of disrespect to the memory of the Bishop. But there is evidence to show that even death, "the mighty leveller," and queller of all strife, did not cool Mr. Wyn's anger towards the Bishop, who had then entered into his rest, where the gentlest praise or the loudest blame could not affect him. The letter of Bishop Parry is a gentle but well-deserved rebuke to Mr. John Wyn.

Inferentially, Mr. Wyn appears to have applied to Bishop Parry for a lease of the tithes of Llanrwst Rectory. At any rate, he seems to have made an effort to ingratiate himself into the good graces of the Bishop, with this object in view ; or, as Morgan put it, "hopynge to make a stave of him to dryve preachers partryges to hys netts."

" Good M[r] Gwyn,

" You needed not this paynes to remove anye conceite of myne. Before y[r] letters, I never heard of

---

[1] *Arch. Camb.*, October 1864, p. 322.

your refusall of subscription unto myen certificate; and now havinge heard of it, I conceave no woorse of you then of a very wyse and sufficient gentleman, whose love in anye good and honest cause I shall be glad to deserve. Touchinge my certieficate, I did sufficientlye knowe, yᵗ no one man in my countrey subscribinge wold much further me, nor anye one man wantinge wold anye thinge hinder me. I am farr from imagininge, yᵗ a gentleman of your place and woorth eyther doth flatter me, or expect bene- fite by me. You have no cause to use yᵉ one, and I have no meanes to afforde yᵉ other ; for as you truelye write, all I have is little enough for yᵉ support of mye owne estate.

"Your hard censure of my predecessor I am very sorye to heare; for I willinglye embrace nothinge ; De mortuis nisi sanctum. Domino suo stetit aut cecidit. And so doe we. God graunt we may stand unto the Lord, unto whose defence I commend us; and with my verye hartye commendationes to y'selfe, I rest

"Your lovinge frend,

"Ric. Asaphen.

"Gresford, 24 Febr. 1605.

"(To the R. Woor, my Lovinge frend, John Gwyn of Gwyder, Esquier, these at Gwyder.)"

Bishop Parry gently reminds Mr. Wyn that his appointment to the Bishopric was not in any way dependent on any certificate from him. That the Bishop was appointed notwithstanding the refusal sufficiently proves this. The writer had evidently in his mind also the controversy between his pre- decessor and Mr. Wyn, and the latter had some lingering hope that a flattering letter might induce Bishop Parry to grant his request. In this he was disappointed, and the closing rebuke in the Bishop's letter was mortifying to the proud spirit of Mr.

Wyn, who had yet to learn humility and wisdom. Even in the few words which Mr. Wyn wrote in the Gwydir *Memoirs*, he could not abstain from showing his pique against the Bishop. Speaking of Morgan, he says—

"He translated the Old Testament into the Welsh tongue before he was Bishop, and while he was Vicar of Llanrhaidr yn mochnant, in the County of Denbigh, whence he had the benefit and help of Bishop Davis and William Salusbury's works, who had done a great part thereof; yet he carried the name of all. He repaired and slated the Chancel of the Cathedral Church of St Asaph, which was a great ruin. He died a poor man. He was a good scholar, both a grecian and hebrician." [1]

"He died a poor man." A high testimony to the character and worth of Bishop Morgan from the pen of an enemy. Mr. Wyn may not have so considered it. In all ages we see an exaggerated desire to obtain wealth, and an excessive admiration of the possession of it, based upon an erroneous belief of the happiness it brings in its train. A man might be as rich as Crœsus, and as miserable as a lost soul; and it is no hard matter to despise human comfort, when we have that which is divine. Bishop Morgan had, in the course of his life, climbed a few rungs of the ladder of promotion. But his *life* was unchanged, in its various circumstances. What he was as Vicar he was as Bishop. His *duties*, as a bishop, were different; his responsibilities greater; his burdens heavier; but these did not bring more happiness

[1] *Memoirs*, p. 96.

in their train. The happiness of his heart depended
on this : that in Christ he had obtained that peace
of mind which the world cannot give, passes all
understanding, and which is given to the richest
and poorest.   That is the condition of true happiness. " Lift up thine eyes to the riches of Heaven,"
says Thomas à Kempis, " and thou shalt see that
all the goods of this life are nothing to be accounted
of.   They are very uncertain, and rather burden-
some than otherwise, because they are never
possessed without anxiety and fear."

Bishop Morgan might, indeed, have died a rich
man, had he chosen to make merchandise of the
Word of God ; but he considered himself promoted
to power, not for his own sake, but for the public
good ; and the endowments of the Church he
regarded as a solemn trust, to be administered for
the spiritual good of the people committed to his
care. This noble spirit, which actuated him in all
he did, is ever refreshing to those who drink of the
waters of salvation freely, through the medium of
his translation of the Word of God. The world
seldom attaches significance to any life except
those of its great heroes, mighty intellects, great
conquerors, and the powerful rich. So it was in
the time of Bishop Morgan. He died, was almost
forgotten, and his name but faintly inscribed on the
annals of history. But it is no small testimony to
his character, and the value of his work, that a
memorial of him is to mark the tercentenary of the
publication of his translation of the Welsh Bible.
Nearly three hundred years have passed away since
Bishop Morgan has been sleeping in earthly dust ;
all his contemporaries have died, and all personal

feelings have passed away, and history can now pronounce her calm verdict upon his existence. Nothing, however, but the light of the Judgment day can reveal, in its true aspect, the value of his labour in the vineyard of his Lord. For ministerial success lies in changed lives, and obedient, humble hearts—unseen work recognized in that Great Day. To those, in all ages, who are engaged in God's work in earnest there is no failure. No work truly done, no sacrifice freely made, was ever made in vain. The cup of cold water given in Christ's name, and for His sake, shall never lose its reward.

Soon after Bishop Morgan's death, a Special Commission was issued by the Crown, to inquire into his assets. The Bishop, as collector of the clerical subsidies in his diocese, appears to have neglected to press the clergy to pay, and to have fallen into arrear. These "subsidies" were the grants made in Convocation upon the tithes. The clergy taxed themselves then. The Crown seized the Bishop's effects. There is in the Public Record Office an "Inventorie of all and singular the goodes and chattells of the Reverend father in god Willm late Bishopp of St. Asaph that were seised by auctorytie and commission of the Right Hō Thomas erle of Dorsit lord Treasurer of England to his mat⁵ use and for the paymᵗ of the Debtes dewe by the said late Bishopp." This document is signed by Dr. John Davies, Rector of Mallwyd; Evan Morgan, Vicar of Llanasa, the Bishop's nephew; John Chambres, of Lleweni, gentleman; and John Price, Head-master of Ruthin Grammar School—the Commissioners.

The whole of the Bishop's effects were valued at

£110 1s. 11d. His furniture was of the plainest kind. The silvers of the palace comprised eight spoons, valued at £2 0s. 5d. All the dishes and plates were of pewter. He appears to have had only one parlour furnished for his own use, with a "longe Dornix carpett and two shorte ons," valued at 9s. 9d.; "a shorte Table and a Frame," valued at 4s.; "two Fayer greene chares, and six greene stooles and xiii Chushons," valued at 46s. 9d. The whole furniture in the Bishop's parlour was valued by the Commission at £3 18s. 3d.

The outdoor effects were of more value. Judging from the inventory of farming implements and farm produce found on the premises, the Bishop appears to have been fond of farming. He possessed "3 working horses, a cow, a roane colt and a black nagg." The Bishop was evidently accustomed to ride, for "the said Bishop's best sadle and brydle" were, among some other effects, in the possession of one John Lloyd, Vaenol, Flintshire, which, as the Commissioners report, they "demanded of the sayde John Lloyd, and which he refused to deliv unto us."

One of the items in the inventory specifies the seizure of tiles and lime, within and without the Cathedral of S. Asaph. These were, no doubt, a portion of the materials connected with the restoration of the chancel; which, as the work was done entirely at the cost of Bishop Morgan, the Commissioners considered as part of his assets.

If Bishop Morgan's wife survived him, she was evidently not provided for.

Glimpses of the social life of the period in which Bishop Morgan lived, reveal the fact that the necessaries of life were not dear, and that house-keeping was comparatively inexpensive. Six chickens cost only 1s. 3d.; the ten hens among Bishop Morgan's effects were valued at 3s.; a whole pig could be purchased for 1s.; but a flitch of cured bacon cost as much as 8s.; a whole mutton could be bought for from 4s. 6d. to 5s.; a duck could be had for 5d.; the five ducks among Bishop Morgan's effects were valued at 1s. 8d., i.e. 4d. each; a goose fetched four times as much. Fish sufficient for a special occasion, when a distinguished guest was to be entertained, did not cost more than 9d.; oatmeal was sold at 16s. the peck, and wheat was bought at Pwllheli for little over 6s. the "hobbett."[1]

The John Lloyd referred to in the "Inventorie" lived at Vaenol Fawr, near S. Asaph, and was Registrar of the diocese, and one of the Bishop's friends. By what authority he seized some of the Bishop's effects, in defiance of the Commissioners, we are not told; but he was probably connected with the Lloyds of Llanfairtalhaiarn, and Bishop Morgan's wife was the widow of one of those Lloyds, and he was probably acting for the widow in this case. He appears to have made a selection before the Commissioners arrived at the Palace, and resolutely refused to allow any interference on the part of his Majesty's representatives. The entire absence of any reference in the inventory to the Bishop's library is noticeable. The only books

---

[1] These particulars are based on a document in the Peniarth Library contributed to the *Archæologia Cambrensis* (Original Documents, p. cix), by the late Mr. W. W. E. Wynne.

named among his effects are " A booke of Statutes at lardge," and " Stowes Chronicle," which Mr. John Lloyd appropriated. This, of course, did not represent the Bishop's library, and he probably made use of the Cathedral library close by. Some of the Bishop's books may possibly have been in the "two packes" which Mr. Lloyd refused to allow the Commissioners to " viewe the particulars of them, so that we coulde not prayse or value the same," and he probably chose " the said Bishop's best sadle and brydle," as a souvenir. If there was a painting or portrait of Morgan at the palace, Lloyd probably took that also. Evan Morgan, the Bishop's nephew, survived his uncle many years, and was promoted by Bishop Parry, Morgan's successor, to the Vicarage of Mold in 1612, was made Rector of Denbigh in 1615, and Prebendary of Meifod in 1617.

It is no reflection on Bishop Morgan's powers of administration to say that he left the diocese in a comparatively unimproved condition. He scarcely held the see of S. Asaph four years, and the diocese was so much out of order when he entered upon its duties, that the mischief done through the avarice and negligence of his predecessors could not be rectified in so short a time. Bishop Richard Parry in a letter to Cecil, dated January 12, 1610—six years after Bishop Morgan's death—gives a very doleful account of the diocese : vicarages in the hands of widows, who employed curates. The original letter, which is in Bishop Parry's own beautiful handwriting, is in the Public Record Office.

Memorial to
Bishop William
Morgan

A D
mdccxci

Exortum est in tenebris
lumen rectis

In memoria aeter
na erit iustus

Scale

Feet

Henry Prothero June 189

APPENDIX A.

A LIST of existing Copies, perfect and imperfect, as far as could be ascertained, of (1) William Salesbury's Welsh New Testament of 1567; (2) Bishop Morgan's Bible of 1588; and Bishop Parry's Bible of 1620.

---

1. WILLIAM SALESBURY'S TESTAMENT.

No.	Names of Owners.	Address.	Description.
1.	Bangor Cathedral Library	Bangor	Wants title-page and dedication. The text wants seventeen leaves in all, eleven of these being at the end. It begins with Bishop Richard Davies' Epistle in Welsh. This copy was presented to the Dean and Chapter by John Roberts, Archdeacon of Merioneth.
2.	William Pamplin	Llandderfel, Corwen	Complete, with title-page.
3.	Bala College Library	Calvinistic Coll., Bala	Incomplete; wants title-page
4.	Peniarth Library	Peniarth, Towyn	Incomplete.
5.	British Museum	B. Museum, Lond.	Quite complete.
6.	Bible Society House	London	Incomplete.
7.	Gwilym Cowlyd	Llanrwst	Fragment only.

WILLIAM SALESBURY'S TESTAMENT (*continued*).

No.	Names of Owners.	Address.	Description.
8.	John Williams	Llandegai, Bangor	Incomplete.
9.	D. G. Goodwin	Buildwas, Iron-bridge, Salop	Title-page wanting, with some other leaves.
10.	The Library of Jesus College, Oxford	Oxford	A complete copy.
11.	Do. Do.	Do.	Duplicate copy, with Middleton's Psalms (1603) bound up with it.
12.	The Rev. Ll. Thomas, M.A., Vice-Principal of Jesus College Oxford	Oxford	An imperfect copy; many pages in most of the New Testament books are missing, and the whole of the Acts; what remains is in good condition, and corresponds exactly in paging and letter-press with the perfect copies at Jesus College Library.
13.	Bodleian Library	Oxford	Perfect copy. [4 : T. 19. Th. Seld.]
14.	Reference Library	Swansea	Imperfect.
15.	Robert Henry Hughes	Post-Office, Four Crosses, Blaenau Ffestiniog	Binding in good condition.
16.	Ven. Archdeacon Thomas	Meifod	Imperfect.

Salesbury's Testament continued in use in churches till 1588, when it was replaced by Bishop Morgan's Bible. From 1567 to 1588 the Second Lesson was read from it. No First Lesson was therefore read for twenty-one years in Welsh at least. If it was read at all, it must have been in English.

2. BISHOP MORGAN'S BIBLE, 1588.

This edition continued in use in churches till 1620, when it was replaced by Bishop Parry's Bible.

No.	Names of Owners.	Address.	Description.
1.	Dean and Chapter of Westminster	Westminster Abbey	Complete copy ; in excellent condition. This is the copy presented by Bishop Morgan himself to the Dean and Chapter of Westminster. It contains, at the end, a sheet of Corrigenda, supposed to be in the handwriting of Dr. Jaspar Gruffydd of Ruthin.
2.	Dean and Chapter of Bangor	Bangor	Wants title-page of Old Testament, and all the pages preceding Gen. xiv. 20 (where it begins). Also of New Testament, all from Jude, verse 9 out, and a few leaves elsewhere. Title-page of New Testament complete. On the cover, inside the fly-leaves, at the beginning are some anonymous remarks upon the history of the work, and upon some criticisms made upon it, in which it is argued that Bishop Morgan made this translation from the Hebrew.
3.	Dean and Chapter of S. Asaph	S. Asaph	Complete. The title-page is partly repaired.
4.	Bala College Library	Calvinistic College, Bala	
5.	John Owen, Tycoch	Carnarvon	Complete, with title-page ; but has been rebound.
6.	Archdeacon of Montgomery	Meifod Vicarage	Wants title-page, last chapter of Job, and the last page of the Book of Revelation.

BISHOP MORGAN'S BIBLE (*continued*).

No.	Names of Owners.	Address.	Description.
7.	Michael D. Jones	The College, Bala	Wants title-page. Has been rebound.
8.	J. C. Evans, M.A.	Grammar School, Bala	Lacks title-page. All the leaves from fifth chapter of Revelation to the end are missing. Binding in excellent condition (original). This copy belonged, at one time, to the late Mr. Richards, Vicar of Meifod.
9.	Miss Hughes	Tai'n-y-Foel, Cerrig-y-Druidion	Very imperfect.
10.	E. W. Evans	Printer, Dolgelly	Title-page missing, and a few leaves at the end of Revelation. Otherwise in good condition.
11.	Bodleian Library	Oxford	Perfect copy. [Bibl. Welsh, 1588, c. i.]
12.	Rev. Thomas Briscoe, D.D.	Holyhead	In a good state. Has been repaired. Wants to Gen. xiv. 19, and from Rev. ii. 12.
13.	Swansea Reference Library	Swansea	Imperfect.
14.	University College	Aberystwyth	
15.	St. David's College	Lampeter	
16.	Rev. D. Morgan	Vicarage, Penrhyn, Deudraeth	
17.	British Museum	London	Wants title-page of Old Testament.

3. BISHOP PARRY'S BIBLE, 1620.

This edition continued in use in churches till 1690, when it was replaced by Bishop Lloyd's Bible, printed in ordinary type.

No.	Names of Owners.	Address.	Description.
1.	Dean and Chapter of Bangor	Bangor Cathedral Library	Complete.
2.	Dean and Chapter of Bangor	Bangor Cathedral Library	Duplicate of above. Wants the title-page of the Old Testament, and all the Calendar and Tables at the beginning. Begins Gen. i. Has a Calendar of Epistles and Gospels for Sundays and Holydays at the end.
3.	Dean and Chapter of S. Asaph	S. Asaph Cathedral Library	Complete ; but has been rebound in vellum.
4.	Edward Morris	Pantsaer, Llanuwchllyn	Title-page worn and damaged. All the Calendars and Tables at the beginning lost, except one page. Binding in excellent condition ; brass clasp, and corner pieces perfect.
5.	Vicar and Churchwardens of Llanllwchhaiarn	Llanllwchhaiarn, Newtown, Montgomeryshire	Wants a leaf of Bishop Morgan's Latin Preface, and the months of the Calendar are not arranged in the proper order. The New Testament is a little more worn than the Old. Otherwise it is a very clean and perfect copy. It has a number of marginal readings in a very legible hand (not the same throughout) correcting the printed text, and harmonizing it with that of a later edition. It is bound in good strong

BISHOP PARRY'S BIBLE (*continued*).

No. Names of Owners.	Address.	Description.
		covers, and had once two clasps ; and is now secure-ly kept in an oak chest, which, it is said, once did service as a Communion Table.
6. Edward Ingman	Queen Street, Leeswood, Mold	Wants title-page ; otherwise in fairly good condition.
7. A. E. Roberts	9, Rossell Road, Blundellsands, near Liverpool	" In good condition."
8. The British Mu-seum	London	This is the copy presented by Bishop Parry to King James I. " A magnificent copy on large paper and in the binding of James I. It is quite complete."
9. W. R. Owen	2, Osmond Terrace Portmadoc	A complete copy.
10. Bodleian Library	Oxford	Perfect copy. [A. 15. 5. Th.]
11. Swansea Refer-ence Library	Swansea	Imperfect.
12. S. David's Cath-edral Library	S. David's	
13. Mrs. Royle	Brynygroes, Bala	Lacks one case of binding.
14. Rev. E. Evans	Llanfihangel Rec-tory, Llanfyllin	Perfect.
15. J. C. Evans, M.A.	Grammar School, Bala	Title page wanting. Leaves from second chapter of S. James' Epistle to the end of Revelation wanting. It has the original binding, but wants repairing. (This copy belonged at one time to the Rev. R. Richards, Vicar of Meifod (formerly of Caerwys).

BISHOP PARRY'S BIBLE (*continued*).

No.	Names of Owners.	Address.	Description.
16.	Rev. W. Roberts	Frondeg, Llanrwst	First chapter of Genesis, ninth chapter of Judges, and from the Epistle to the Colossians to Revelation (both inclusive) are missing.
17.	Wynn Finch, Esq.	Voelas Hall, Pentre Voelas	Complete copy.
		Hafody Drefisaf, Pentre Voelas	Complete copy.
18.	Vicar and Church-wardens of Pentre Voelas	Pentre Voelas, Bettws-y-coed	An imperfect copy, kept in the parish chest.
19.	E. W. Evans	Printer, Dolgelly	Imperfect copy.
20.	Rev. John Hughes	Talysarn, Carnarvon	From the latter part of the fourteenth chapter of Revelation to the end missing. Otherwise in good condition.
21.	R. Rhys Jones	Board School, Denbigh	Complete copy. Title-page missing.
22.	E. Pryse	Bodedern, Anglesey	"In good condition."
23.	David Morgan	8, Segontium Terrace, Carnarvon	The edges of the leaves of the first twenty chapters of Genesis are very much worn at the edges, and some words and portions of words lost. From Genesis xx. to the end of Revelation complete, with exception of a few of the closing verses of latter.

CHRONOLOGY OF CHIEF EVENTS IN THE LIFE AND TIMES OF BISHOP MORGAN.

A.D.

1547 *Birth of Bishop Morgan.*

1547 First printed book in the Welsh language published.

1547 First Book of Homilies printed.

1547-53 EDWARD VI.

1549 First Book of Common Prayer published.

1550 Salesbury's *Brief and Plain Introduction*, &c. to the Welsh language published.

1551 Salesbury's Welsh translation of Epistles and Gospels published.

1552 XLII. Articles of Religion published.

1552 Second Book of Common Prayer published.

1553 Sir John Wyn of Gwydir born.

1553-8 MARY.

1555 Bishop Ferrar of S. David's burnt at Carmarthen.

1555 Extermination of Gwylliaid Cochion Mawddwy.

1556 Archbishop Cranmer burnt.

1557 Bangor Grammar School founded.

1558 William Nichol and Rowlins White burnt at Haverfordwest.

1558 Invention of Postal arrangements.

1558—1603 ELIZABETH.

1559 Publication of Humphrey Llwyd's *History of Wales*.

1559 Consecration of Archbishop Parker.

1559 Consecration of Rowland Meyrick to the see of Bangor.

1560 The Pope offers to sanction the Reformation on acknowledgment of his supremacy.

1560 Bishop Jewell preached his great sermon at S. Paul's Cross.

1560 Consecration of Jewell, Richard Davies, and Thos. Young.

1561 Translation of Bishop Davies from S. Asaph to S. David's.

1561 Dr. Gabriel Goodman becomes Dean of Westminster.

1562 XXXVIII. Articles of Religion published.

1562 Jewell's *Apology* published.

1563 Act of Parliament passed for translating Bible and Prayer-Book into the Welsh language.

1563 Second Book of Homilies published (written by Bishop Jewell).

1564 *William Morgan matriculates at Cambridge.*

1566 Nicholas Robinson consecrated to Bangor.

1566 Hugh Jones consecrated to Llandaff.

1566 Birth of Sir William Jones.

1567 Salesbury's Welsh Translation of the New Testament published.

1567 Welsh Translation of Book of Common Prayer published.

A. D.

1567 First Welsh Grammar by Dr. Griffith Roberts published.

1567 *Athrawiaeth Gristionogol* published.

1567 *William Morgan graduated at Cambridge.*

1568 Parker's Bible published.

1569 The Pope excommunicates Queen Elizabeth.

1570 Dr. John Davies, Mallwyd, born.

1571 *Morgan takes the degree of M.A.*

1571 XXXIX. Articles of Religion put forward.

1571 ? *Morgan ordained Deacon.*

1572 ? *Morgan ordained Priest.*

1572 Edmund Prys became Rector of Maentwrog.

1573 Founding of Jesus College, Oxford.

1573 Consecration of Bp. William Hughes to S. Asaph.

1575 *Morgan appointed Vicar of Welshpool.*

1576 Edmund Prys became Archdeacon of Merioneth.

1578 *Morgan appointed Vicar of Llanrhaiadr - ym - mochnant.*

1578 *Morgan takes the degree of B.D.*

1578 *Is appointed University preacher.*

1579 *Morgan made Rector of Llanfyllin.*

1580 (April 16) Archdeacon Prys made Rector of Llanenddwyn.

1581 Death of Bp. Richard Davies

1583 John Whitgift made Archbishop of Canterbury.

1583 *Morgan takes the degree of D.D.*

A. D.

1583 ? *Is summoned before Archbishop Whitgift.*

1583 ? Made Chaplain to the Archbishop.

1584 Richard Hooker appointed Master of the Temple.

1585 Importation of potatoes and tobacco into England.

1585 Death of Bishop Robinson of Bangor.

1586 New Edition (corrected) of Welsh Prayer-Book published.

1587 Martin Marprelate Tracts published.

1588 Destruction of Spanish Armada.

1588 *Morgan's Translation of the Welsh Bible published.*

1590 "Ieuan Tew's" Cywydd to Dr. Morgan written.

1592 Dr. John Davydd Rhys' *Grammatical Institutes* published.

1593 Penal Statutes against Romanists and Nonconformists enacted.

1593 ? Death of Wm. Salesbury.

1593 Execution of John Penry.

1594 Dr. John Davies, Mallwyd, ordained.

1594 *Dr. Morgan made Sinecure Rector of Denbigh.*

1594 Morrus Cyffin's translation of Jewell's *Apology* into Welsh published.

1595 (July 20) *Dr. Morgan consecrated Bishop of Llandaff.*

1595 Dr. Richard Vaughan consecrated Bishop of Bangor

1595 Lambeth Articles published

1595 Ruthin Grammar School founded by Dean Goodman.

A D.

1595 *Egluryn Ffraethineb* published.

1596 Bishop Bellott died.

1597 Bishop Vaughan translated from Bangor to Chester.

1598 Dr. David Powell, Vicar of Ruabon, died.

1599 Dr. Richard Parry made Dean of Bangor.

1600 Wm. Cynwal died. Buried at Penmachno.

1600 Death of Bishop William Hughes of S. Asaph.

1601 *Translation of Bp. Morgan to S. Asaph.* (Elected by the Chapter, July 21.)

1601 (June 21) Death of Dr. Gabriel Goodman, Dean of Westminster.

1602 Ordination of Rhys Prichard, afterwards the famous Vicar of Llandovery.

1602 Archdeacon Prys made

A. D.

Canon of S. Asaph (Oct. 8) by Bishop Morgan.

1603-25 JAMES I.

1603 Edward Cyffin's translation of a portion of the Book of Psalms into Welsh published.

1603 Millenary Petition presented to King James.

1603 *Dispute between Bishop Morgan and Mr. John Wyn of Gwydir.*

1604 Hampton Court Conference.

1604 (Feb. 29) Death of Archbishop Whitgift.

1604 Bishop Vaughan translated from Chester to London.

1604 Canons Ecclesiastical published.

1604 Dr. John Davies becomes Rector of Mallwyd.

1604 *Death of Bishop Morgan at the Palace, S. Asaph, Sept.* 10.

APPENDIX B.

KEY TO MONUMENT.

THE names indicate the position of the Statues in the niches of the National Monument erected to Bishop Morgan on the north side of the Cathedral of S. Asaph, and the numbers the degree of prominence which the helpers in the work of translating the Bible into Welsh occupy; special prominence being, of course, given to the Statue of Bishop Morgan, and of the niche that holds it, facing the main street of the city of S. Asaph.

Around the base of the monument is this inscription in English—

"A.D. 1588—1888.

" This Tercentenary Memorial of the translation of the Bible into Welsh by Bishop Morgan was erected by National Subscription."

Under each Statue are inscriptions in the Welsh language, of which the following are translations.

(1)

WILLIAM MORGAN, D.D.
Translator of the Bible into Welsh.
1588.
Vicar of Llanrhaiadr yn Mochnant   1578—1595.
Bishop of Llandaff   .   .   .   1595—1601.
Bishop of S. Asaph   .   .   .   1601—1604.
Died, September 10, 1604.

" Religio, nisi vulgari lingua edoceatur, ignota latitabit."—*Bishop Morgan.*

(2)

WILLIAM SALESBURY.

Translator of the New Testament and of the Book of Common Prayer into the Welsh language.

1567.

"Eich car o waet yn ol y cnawt a'ch brawt ffydd in Christ Iesu."

W.S.

(3)

RICHARD DAVIES, D.D.

A Translator of a portion of the Testament of 1567.

Bishop of S. Asaph   .   .   1560—1561.
Bishop of S. David's   .   .   1561—1581.

"Yr Anrhydeddus Dat . . . ail Dewi Menew."—W. S.

(4)

THOMAS HUET.

Precentor of S. David's.

A Translator of a portion of the Testament of 1567.

(5)

GABRIEL GOODMAN, D.D.

Dean of Westminster.

One who was of no little help to Bishop Morgan.

(6)

EDMUND PRYS.

Archdeacon of Merioneth.

A Helper to Bishop Morgan.

The Author of the Metrical Psalms in Welsh, 1621.

(7)

RICHARD PARRY, D.D.

Bishop of S. Asaph   .   .   1604—1623.

Author of the Revised Version of the Welsh Bible.[1]

1620.

(8)

JOHN DAVIES, D.D.[2]

Rector of Mallwyd.

A Helper to Bishop Parry.

[1] He died Sep. 26, 1623, and was buried in S. Asaph Cathedral.
[2] He died May 15, 1644, and was buried in Mallwyd Church.

PUBLICATIONS

OF THE

Society for Promoting Christian Knowledge.

A Dictionary of the Church of England.

By the Rev. EDWARD L. CUTTS. With numerous Woodcuts.
Crown 8vo. 7s. 6d.

Aids to Prayer.

By the Rev. DANIEL MOORE. Printed in red and black.
Post 8vo. 1s. 6d.

Being of God (Six Addresses on the).

By C. J. ELLICOTT, D.D., Bishop of Gloucester and Bristol.
Small Post 8vo. 1s. 6d.

Bible Places; or, The Topography of the Holy Land.

By the Rev. CANON TRISTRAM. With Map and numerous
Woodcuts. Crown 8vo. 4s.

Called to be Saints.

The Minor Festivals Devotionally Studied. By CHRISTINA
G. ROSSETTI, Author of "Seek and Find." Post 8vo. 5s.

Case for "Establishment" stated (The).

By the Rev. T. MOORE, M.A. Post 8vo. *Paper boards.* 6d.

Christians under the Crescent in Asia.

By the Rev. E. L. CUTTS, B.A. With numerous Illustrations. Crown 8vo. 5s.

Daily Readings for a Year.

By ELIZABETH SPOONER. Crown 8vo. 3s. 6d.

Devotional (A) Life of Our Lord.

By the Rev. EDWARD L. CUTTS, B.A., Author of " Pastoral Counsels," &c. Post 8vo. 5s.

Golden Year (The).

Thoughts for every month. Original and Selected. By EMILY C. ORR, Author of " Thoughts for Working Days." Printed in red and black. Post 8vo. 1s. 6d.

Gospels (The Four).

Arranged in the Form of an English Harmony, from the Text of the Authorized Version. By the Rev. J. M. FULLER. With Analytical Table of Contents and Four Maps. 1s.

Holy Eucharist, The Evidential Value of the.

Being the Boyle Lectures for 1879 and 1880. By the Rev. G. F. MACLEAR, D.D. Crown 8vo. Cloth boards, 4s.

Land of Israel (The).

A Journal of Travel in Palestine, undertaken with special reference to its Physical Character. By the Rev. Canon TRISTRAM. With Two Maps and numerous Illustrations. Large Post 8vo. Cloth boards, 10s. 6d.

Lectures on the Historical and Dogmatical Position of the Church of England.

By the Rev. W. BAKER, D.D. Post 8vo. Cloth boards, 1s. 6d.

Paley's Evidences.

A New Edition, with Notes, Appendix, and Preface. By the Rev. E. A. LITTON. Post 8vo. *Cloth boards, 4s.*

Paley's Horæ Paulinæ.

A New Edition, with Notes, Appendix, and Preface. By the late Rev. J. S. HOWSON, D.D. Post 8vo. *Cloth boards, 3s.*

Peace with God.

A Manual for the Sick. By the Rev. E. BURBIDGE, M.A. Post 8vo. *Cloth boards, 1s. 6d.*

"Perfecting Holiness."

By the Rev. E. L. CUTTS, B.A. Post 8vo. *Cloth boards, 2s. 6d.*

Plain Words for Christ.

Being a Series of Readings for Working Men. By the late Rev. R. G. DUTTON. Post 8vo. *Cloth boards, 1s.*

Readings on the First Lessons for Sundays and Chief Holy Days.

According to the New Table. By the Rev. PETER YOUNG. Crown 8vo. *In two volumes, 6s.*

Sinai and Jerusalem; or, Scenes from Bible Lands.

Consisting of Coloured Photographic Views of Places mentioned in the Bible, including a Panoramic View of Jerusalem, with Descriptive Letterpress. By the Rev. F. W. HOLLAND, M.A. Demy 4to. *Cloth, bevelled boards, gilt edges, 6s.*

Some Chief Truths of Religion.

By the Rev. EDWARD L. CUTTS, B.A., Author of "St. Cedd's Cross," &c. Crown 8vo. *Cloth boards, 2s. 6d.*

Thoughts for Men and Women.

THE LORD'S PRAYER. By EMILY C. ORR. Post 8vo. *Limp cloth*, 1s.

Thoughts for Working Days.

Original and Selected. By EMILY C. ORR. Post 8vo. *Limp cloth*, 1s.

Time Flies; a Reading Diary.

By CHRISTINA G. ROSSETTI. Post 8vo. *Cloth boards*, 2s. 6d.

Turning Points of English Church History.

By the Rev. EDWARD L. CUTTS, B.A., Vicar of Holy Trinity, Haverstock Hill. Crown 8vo. *Cloth boards*, 3s. 6d.

Turning Points of General Church History.

By the Rev. E. L. CUTTS, B.A., Author of " Pastoral Counsels." Crown 8vo. *Cloth boards*, 5s.

LONDON :

NORTHUMBERLAND AVENUE, CHARING CROSS, W.C. ;

43, QUEEN VICTORIA STREET, E.C.

BRIGHTON : 135, NORTH STREET.

.

CPSIA information can be obtained at www.ICGtesting.com
Printed in the USA
BVOW07s1110060514

352713BV00011B/747/P